Winning Mindset for Athletes

Unlock Peak Performance, Boost Confidence, and Achieve Consistent Success

Rashaun Simonise

© **Copyright 2024 - All rights reserved.**

The content contained within this book may not be reproduced, duplicated or transmitted without direct written permission from the author or the publisher.

Under no circumstances will any blame or legal responsibility be held against the publisher, or author, for any damages, reparation, or monetary loss due to the information contained within this book, either directly or indirectly.

Legal Notice:

This book is copyright protected. It is only for personal use. You cannot amend, distribute, sell, use, quote or paraphrase any part, or the content within this book, without the consent of the author or publisher.

Disclaimer Notice:

Please note the information contained within this document is for educational and entertainment purposes only. All effort has been executed to present accurate, up to date, reliable, complete information. No warranties of any kind are declared or implied. Readers acknowledge that the author is not engaged in the rendering of legal, financial, medical or professional advice. The content within this book has been derived from various sources. Please consult a licensed professional before attempting any techniques outlined in this book.

By reading this document, the reader agrees that under no circumstances is the author responsible for any losses, direct or indirect, that are incurred as a result of the use of the information contained within this document, including, but not limited to, errors, omissions, or inaccuracies.

Table of Contents

INTRODUCTION 1
    WHO THIS BOOK IS FOR 3
    THE REAL POWER OF THE GAME 5
    THE JOURNEY AHEAD 6

CHAPTER 1: THE WINNING MINDSET 9
    THE ELITE ATHLETE'S SECRET 9
    JUST GOTTA HAVE FAITH 10
    MENTAL MONEY 11
    BUILDING BULLETPROOF CONFIDENCE 13
        The Preparation Factor *13*
        The Adversity Advantage *13*
        The Competition Mindset *13*
    THE ART OF CONTROLLED AGGRESSION 14
    THE PSYCHOLOGY OF DOMINANCE 15
    BUILDING THE BEAST 15
    THE UNCOMFORTABLE TRUTH 16
    THE PRICE OF GREATNESS 16
    YOUR SECOND HOME 17
    THE NO-EXCUSES ZONE 17
        Learn to Set Goals *18*
    DREAMS VS. GOALS 18
        Making It Real *19*
    THE COMPLETE PLAYER 20
    THE FINAL PUSH 20
    BUILDING YOUR MENTAL TOOLKIT 21
    THE POWER OF VISUALIZATION 21
        Game-Day Mental Preparation *23*
        Focus: Your Secret Weapon *24*
        Building Mental Endurance *24*
    THE CHAMPION'S MINDSET IN ACTION 25
    LEARNING FROM THE GREATS 26
        Jerry Rice *26*
        Tom Brady *27*
        When Champions Fail *27*
    YOUR DAILY CHAMPIONSHIP PRACTICE 28
        Building Unshakeable Mental Toughness *29*
    YOUR NEXT STEPS 30
    YOUR ACTION ITEMS 30

The Academic Connection 31

CHAPTER 2: GRADES MATTER 33

The Student in Student-Athlete 34
A Hard Lesson Learned 35
The Reality Check 36
The Painful Truth 37
The Real World of Athletic Recruitment 37
Making Choices That Matter 40
The Choices That Define Us 40
The Character Test 41
Beyond the Classroom 42
The Growth Mindset 42
Making Your Own Choices 43
When Talent Isn't Enough 44
The Price of Academic Neglect 44
The Narrow Window 45
The Real Cost 45
Beyond Football 46
The Reality Check 47
Breaking the Cycle 47
Building Academic Success 48
Time Management: Your Most Valuable Life Skill 48
   The Power Block System 49
   Making Every Minute Count 49
Study Skills That Score in Life 50
   The Focus Formation 50
   The Note-Taking Playbook 50
   Preparation Principles 51
Building Your Success Network 52
   Authority Figure Relationships 52
   Support System Utilization 52
The Champion's Daily Routine 53
   Morning Excellence 53
   Peak Performance Time 53
   Evening Mastery 54
The Extra Mile: Excellence in Everything 54
Resources at Your Disposal 55
   Your Academic Support Team 55
The Technology Playbook 57
   Study Apps That Score 57
   Organization Tools: Your Academic Equipment 58
   Time Management Tech 58
Making It All Work Together 58

THE LONG GAME 60
    Life Beyond the Lines 60
    Building Your Professional Playbook... 60
    The Education Advantage 61
    Your Post-Playing Options 61
    The Compound Effect... 62
    The Ultimate Victory 63
THE FINAL WARNING 63
KEY TAKEAWAYS 63
YOUR ACTION ITEMS 64
THE BRIDGE TO EXCELLENCE 65

CHAPTER 3: TRAINING LIKE A CHAMPION 67

THE TRUTH ABOUT GREATNESS... 67
THE FOUNDATION PERIOD 68
    Building Your Base 69
    Understanding the Training Phases 69
    Setting Realistic Goals.. 69
    Mental Preparation 70
    The Foundation Mindset.. 71
NUTRITION AND HYDRATION 72
THE SCIENCE OF FUELING A CHAMPION 73
    Meal Timing: The When Matters as Much as the What 73
    Portion Control for Performance.. 74
    Supplementation: The Truth 74
    Common Nutrition Mistakes and How to Avoid Them........................... 75
    Creating Your Nutrition Game Plan 76
DAILY STRUCTURE FOR SUCCESS 76
    Beyond the Basic Schedule... 77
    The Success System.. 79
    The Off-Season Blueprint 81
THE EVOLUTION OF A CHAMPION 81
    Month 1: The Foundation 82
    Month 2: The Builder 82
    Month 3: The Power Phase 83
POSITION-SPECIFIC EXCELLENCE 83
TRACKING YOUR TRANSFORMATION... 84
SPEED DEVELOPMENT 85
    The Science of Speed.. 85
PRESEASON PREPARATION 87
    Mastering Your Craft 88
    The Mental Game 90
    Integration Work 90
IN-SEASON EXCELLENCE 91

  The Championship Routine 92
  Recovery Mastery 97
 THE CHAMPION'S MINDSET 99
  Beyond the Physical 99

CHAPTER 4: NAVIGATING RECRUITMENT **101**

 THE TRUTH ABOUT YOUR JOURNEY 101
 THE MODERN RECRUITMENT LANDSCAPE 104
 THE NEW REALITY 104
  The Transfer Portal Effect 105
  The Politics of Recruiting 105
  The Truth About Recruiting Services 106
  The Competition Reality 106
 STANDING OUT FROM THE CROWD 107
 CREATING DOMINANT FILM 108
  Position-By-Position Excellence 108
  The Physical Presence Factor 109
  Beyond the Measurables 110
  Creating Your Signature 111
  The Art of Film 111
  Creating Your Story on Film 112
 BUILDING YOUR RECRUITING PROFILE 115
  The Academic Foundation 116
  Beyond Basic Numbers 116
  The Physical Profile 117
  The Development Story 117
  Putting It All Together 118
 COACH COMMUNICATION STRATEGY 119
  The Art of Coach Communication 119
  The Follow-up Formula 120
  Managing the Process 121
 THE REALITY OF RECRUITMENT 122
  Staying Organized Amid the Chaos 122
  Planning Campus Visits 123
  Managing Your Timeline 123
  Making the Right Decision 123
  When Things Don't Go as Planned 124
 HANDLING ADVERSITY 124
  The Reality of Rejection 125
  Managing Expectations 126
  Staying Motivated Through Adversity 127
  Finding Alternative Paths 127
  The Mental Game 128
 THE BIGGER PICTURE 128

    Making the Right Choice 129
    UNDERSTANDING PROGRAM FIT 129
        The Development Factor 131
        Academic and Cultural Alignment 131
    THE DECISION PROCESS 132
    THE FINAL MESSAGE 132
    BEYOND RECRUITMENT 133

CONCLUSION 135

    THE MINDSET OF CHAMPIONS 135
    LIFE'S PLAYBOOK 137
    THE FOUNDATION OF EXCELLENCE 137
    THE POWER OF PROCESS 138
    THE CHAMPIONSHIP MINDSET 139
        The Art of Opportunity 140
    BEYOND THE FIELD 140
        Leadership Born in Battle 140
        The Ultimate Team Sport 141
        Rising Above 141
    YOUR BIGGER IMPACT 141
    YOUR TIME IS NOW 143
        The Power of Now 143
        Building Your Legacy 144
    THE FINAL CHALLENGE 144

REFERENCES 147

    IMAGE REFERENCES 150

Introduction

Fourth quarter. Two minutes left. You're down by six.

Your legs are burning. Your lungs are on fire. Every muscle in your body is screaming at you to quit. But champions aren't made in the moments when everything's easy. They're made right here, in the moments that test not just your body but your soul.

This is football. Not just the game you see on TV. Not just the highlights and the glory. This is the real game, the one that transforms dreamers into achievers and ordinary players into legends.

I've lived through this transformation. I've felt the pain of early morning workouts when everyone else was sleeping. I've tasted the disappointment of setbacks and the sweet victory of proving doubters wrong. I've seen how this game can take a kid from nothing and give him everything—if he's willing to pay the price.

But here's what most people don't understand about football: The game gives you nothing. It only offers opportunities—opportunities that you have to be ready to seize. Opportunities that you have to earn with every rep, every sprint, every study session, and every moment when you choose the hard right over the easy wrong.

Let me tell you a truth about football that most people don't understand: It's not just about what happens between those white lines. It's about who you become in the process of chasing greatness.

If you're reading this, you're probably thinking about or already playing the game of football, or maybe you're just a major fan of the game. Before I get into anything, I need to explain what this game means to me. At the end of the day, it's a kids' game, but the crazy part is that this game can bring you anything you can dream of if you work hard enough. The game can lead you to places you'd never see without it and show you new experiences with countless people along the way.

The game will bring you *power* in the public eye. You will walk into rooms, and people will stare and ask for pictures and even autographs. You will get discounts, celebrity treatment, and even free stuff along your journey. The game provides its own lifestyle that you won't find outside of being an athlete.

Through all those materialistic things, the most important one the game will bring you is the competitive mindset you develop along the way. Competing against yourself daily to chase perfection, knowing you will never be perfect. Competing against your teammates in practice and, of course, competing against other elite athletes on game day. When I step on that field and tie up my Nikes, all my problems seem to go into hiding, and suddenly, nothing matters but that very moment—that very rep or that very route. The only time in my life when my mind is completely clear. The field is my happy place, and there's nowhere I'd rather be. Through 22 years of football, the game has given me everything I could ask for, but the most important thing along the journey was the lessons I learned from making mistakes.

What were the biggest lessons I learned, you might ask? There are two equally important ones:

- **Number 1:** The game will not love you back. Millions of football players are competing for fewer than 3,000 spots. You do the math. The NFL should stand for *Not For Long* because there's always a younger, faster, and bigger athlete waiting to take your position for less money. You have to make the most of it while you can because it only lasts so long before your clock runs out. The journey is full of windows that you *must* capitalize on. Otherwise, it can blow your chances.

- **Number 2:** You get out what you put in. Do you want success? Do you want to be the best at what you do? Do you want to make it to that next level? Everything in football is *earned*, not given. If you give half effort during training, you'll only be half the player you could be. You have to constantly sharpen and work on your skills day in and day out. There is no offseason. Nobody wakes up in the morning and runs a 4.4. Behind that, there are countless hours of training, sacrifices, and pain. You have to work for every single thing you want to achieve in your career. All the little things add up to unleash on game day. The motto is "Stay ready so you ain't gotta get ready" because anything can happen at *any time*.

Who This Book Is For

This book is for dreamers ready to become doers. For those who don't just want to play the game, but want to master it. For those who understand that greatness isn't given but earned through sweat, sacrifice, and an unwavering commitment to excellence.

This book is for:

- the player staying late after practice, running routes in the dark, and chasing perfection when no one's watching
- the athlete who knows they're capable of more and is hungry to prove it
- the high school star who dreams of playing college ball and needs to know what it takes exactly
- the student-athlete determined to dominate in the classroom as hard as they do on the field
- the young competitor looking for an edge that goes beyond just physical talent
- the player who's been told they're too small, too slow, or not good enough and is ready to prove everyone wrong
- those who want more than just motivation; they want transformation
- players who understand that mental toughness is what separates champions from everyone else
- anyone who's ever felt their football dreams slipping away and needs the blueprint to grab them back

Above all, this book is especially for those ready to do the work that others won't. Not just the physical grind that everyone talks about, but the mental work: the deep, challenging, sometimes uncomfortable work that turns good players into great ones and great ones into legends.

What you're holding isn't just a book about football; it's a road map to becoming the best version of yourself. It's for anyone who's ever looked at the players on TV and thought, *That could be me.* Because it can be. But only if you're willing to pay the price.

This isn't for:

- Players looking for shortcuts to success—there aren't any.
- Those who run from hard truths—this book is full of them.
- Anyone who thinks talent alone is enough—it never is.
- People who want results without responsibility—that's not how this works.
- Those not ready to face their weaknesses—because that's where growth begins.
- Players who quit when things get hard—because they will get hard.

But if you're ready to do the following, then this book isn't just for you; it's your blueprint for success:

- Push past your limits every single day.
- Learn from every failure and come back stronger.
- Build championship habits that last a lifetime.
- Develop a mindset that can't be broken.
- Transform your potential into an unstoppable performance.
- Make your mark on the game.
- Prove the doubters wrong.

- Become someone others look up to.
- Create a legacy that lasts.

This isn't about quick fixes or temporary changes. *This is about building something that lasts.* Something that matters. Something that changes not just how you play the game but how you attack every challenge life throws at you.

The question isn't whether this book is for you. The question is: Are you ready for what this book demands of you?

Because if you are, let's get to work.

The Real Power of the Game

Think about every great player you've ever watched. Every champion you've ever admired. Every success story that inspired you. Behind each one, there's more than just talent. There's a story of transformation. A story of someone who let the game mold them into something greater than they imagined possible.

This game will test you in ways nothing else can:

- when it's the fourth quarter, and your body is screaming to quit
- when it's 5 a.m., and your bed is begging you to stay
- when everyone else is partying, but you're studying film
- when doubt creeps in, but you have to believe anyway

These moments? They're not just football moments. They're life-defining moments. They're the times when you discover who you really are and what you're truly capable of.

The Journey Ahead

Listen up because what I'm about to share isn't just another collection of motivational quotes or feel-good stories. This is real. This is raw. This is what separates the players who make it from those who just dream about it.

Every champion you've ever admired started exactly where you are right now. With a dream. With hunger. With something to prove. But they did something different than everyone else: They committed to the process. Not just for a day, not just for a season, but for life.

In these pages, you're going to learn what it really takes from someone who's been in the trenches, faced the doubts, pushed through the pain, and come out the other side stronger.

In light of the aforementioned, we're going to break down the following:

- how to build mental toughness that doesn't break under pressure

- the real secrets to staying focused when others lose their way

- what commitment actually looks like—not what people think it looks like

- the daily habits that separate champions from everyone else

- how to turn your biggest dreams into your reality

But let me be clear: This isn't just about football. This is about building something bigger than yourself. This is about becoming someone who doesn't just talk about greatness but lives it. Every. Single. Day.

Do you see those guys playing under the bright lights on Sundays? They all started somewhere. They all faced moments of doubt. They all had people tell them they couldn't make it. But they had something special: not talent, not luck, but an unshakeable belief in themselves and a willingness to work harder than everyone else.

That's what this book is about. It's your blueprint. Your road map. Your guide to not just playing the game but mastering it. Not just dreaming big but achieving big.

The clock is already ticking. Every second that passes is one you'll never get back. Every day you wait is a day someone else is getting better. Every moment of hesitation is a moment of opportunity lost.

So, here's my question to you: Are you ready? Not just ready to read but ready to work. Ready to push. Ready to sacrifice. Ready to become something greater than you ever imagined possible?

Because the game isn't waiting. The field isn't waiting. Your future isn't waiting.

Your journey starts now.

What's it going to be?

Chapter 1:
The Winning Mindset

Every championship. Every record. Every victory that's ever been celebrated under stadium lights started in the same place: the mind. Before the trophies, before the glory, before the roar of the crowd, there was a decision. A moment when an athlete looked in the mirror and chose greatness.

That's what this chapter is about. Not just thinking like a winner but transforming your mind into an unstoppable force that propels you toward your goals. Because in football, like in life, your mindset isn't just part of the game; it *is* the game.

The Elite Athlete's Secret

Walk into any high school weight room, and you'll find athletes with dreams. Some dream of Friday night glory. Others of college scholarships. A select few dare to dream of NFL stardom. But here's what separates the ones who make it from the ones who don't: It's not just about how bad you want it; it's about what you're willing to do for it.

Elite athletes understand something that others don't: Talent is just a starting point. The real difference-maker is what happens between your ears. It's the voice that gets you up at 5 a.m. when your body is screaming for more sleep. It's the determination that keeps you running routes long after practice has ended. It's the mental toughness that turns *I can't* into *I must*.

Mental toughness isn't something you're born with; it's something you build, rep by rep, day by day, choice by choice. And it starts with a story about belief.

First and foremost, if you really want to hit that next level and beyond, it starts with your mindset. Let me tell you a short story. When I was in 11th grade, we had a split class with the seniors, and my friend group and I were discussing our goals for graduation and which schools we were looking at. I firmly expressed that my goal was to get a Division I scholarship, so I needed to plan my classes for the following year accordingly. I then told them that I needed to go DI because I was going to the NFL. At the time, I thought it was the only way because I had never seen anyone do it as a receiver. A senior girl looked at me and told me verbatim, "You're not going to the NFL, Rashaun. Be realistic."

This is a moment I've never forgotten because I realized right then that I sounded crazy, and from her perspective, it was unimaginable. The point of this story is that I had the goal of making it to the NFL for as long as I can remember and never, for one second, doubted my belief. I didn't know how I was going to get there, which direction to go, or if it was even possible, but I could not convince myself otherwise. No plan B, no side hustle, no CFL. *"I'm going to play in the NFL."*

Six years later, I signed with the Cincinnati Bengals on a free-agent contract and had the first-ever pro day for a wide receiver in Canada at the University of Calgary. Six NFL teams flew to a different country to watch only me in a stadium that seated 35,000 people. I strongly believe that if I had never believed in my heart that I could do it, I don't think I would've fought through everything to get there. I worked like there was no tomorrow, afraid that one day off would be the difference between me making it or not.

Just Gotta Have Faith

Think about that moment. A young athlete declares his dream, and the world rushes to tell him he's crazy. It's a scene that plays out thousands of times across the country. But here's what most people miss: Those moments of doubt aren't obstacles; they're opportunities. Every "no" you hear is a chance to strengthen your "yes."

The science behind the belief is fascinating. When you truly believe in something, your brain literally rewires itself to help you achieve it. Every time you reinforce your belief, every time you visualize success, you're not just dreaming; you're programming your mind for achievement.

But belief isn't just about positive thinking. It's about positive *doing*.

What I'm trying to say is that if football is your goal, you have to be willing to do *whatever* it takes to accomplish it. I slept on couches, had no money in a different country, and even risked being away from my family to get the proper training I needed. I never had a summer vacation or any vacation until my 21st birthday, after I made it.

Dream so big that regular people can't even comprehend what you're trying to do. But don't get it twisted... the higher the level you want to reach, the more work you'll have to put in, and that's just inevitable. Don't let other people's doubts get in the way of your dreams and your belief in yourself. You will be tested more and more as you go, but will you break and give up, or will you keep working and go harder? If you don't love the game, you won't have the will to push through at a certain point.

Mental Money

Here's what most people don't understand about high-level athletics: It's not about being fearless; it's about being afraid and doing it anyway. It's about turning pressure into power, doubt into determination, and challenges into opportunities.

Think about the greatest athletes you've ever watched. Michael Jordan. Jerry Rice. Tom Brady. What sets them apart isn't just their physical gifts; it's their ability to perform under pressure. To want the ball when the game is on the line. To believe, deep in their souls, that they're going to win even when the odds say otherwise.

This kind of mental strength isn't magic. It's methodical. It's built through the following:

- controlled pressure training

- putting yourself in high-stakes situations during practice
- creating gamelike scenarios when training
- learning to thrive under stress, not just survive it
- mental rehearsal
    - visualizing success in vivid detail
    - programming your mind for peak performance
    - building muscle memory through mental practice
- emotional regulation
    - managing adrenaline under pressure
    - channeling nervous energy into focused power
    - maintaining composure when others lose theirs

Now that we talked a bit about mindset, and before we dive into other things, there's another aspect I want to address regarding mindset when it's time to play: confidence.

Confidence comes from the work you put in during the offseason. I knew that I was so prepared and that there was nothing anybody I lined up against could do to stop me. Don't get me wrong, some guys would compete and possibly slow me down a bit, but they would not shut me out. Think about those days when you left the gym or field and couldn't walk properly or those times you threw up halfway through the workout but kept going. It all leads up to game time. Once you gain this confidence, you will truly find the love you have for the game. In this setting, game time becomes fun when you know you can change the game at any moment.

I took it as disrespect from anybody who tried to step up and line up against me. Do you really think you and I belong on the same field? You haven't put in the hours like I did. You haven't paid your dues to the game like me. Straight like that.

Building Bulletproof Confidence

Let's break down what real confidence looks like because there's a big difference between confidence and arrogance. Confidence is earned in the dark when nobody's watching. It's built through the following:

The Preparation Factor

- Every extra rep adds to your confidence bank.
- Each film study session sharpens your mental edge.
- Every drop of sweat is an investment in your self-belief.

The Adversity Advantage

Most players try to avoid difficult situations. Champions seek them out. Why? Because they understand that:

- Adversity builds mental calluses.
- Challenges create opportunities for growth.
- Pressure situations prepare oneself for bigger moments.

The Competition Mindset

True confidence isn't about believing you'll never fail. It's about knowing you can handle whatever comes your way. This means:

- embracing challenges as opportunities
- viewing setbacks as feedback, not failure

- understanding that confidence is a skill you can develop

The game-day field is a shark tank. It's eat or be eaten. You have to want to destroy your opponent. Line up on me at your own risk. Every single time that whistle blows, you have to be willing to go all out, every single play, literally like it's your last. *Sacrifice* your body for the team when necessary, and be able to look yourself in the mirror at the end of the game and honestly say you left it all out there. Every play is an opportunity to make a play, whether it's a catch, a block, or even a route to set up a concept later in the game. When it's time to block, someone in the opposite jersey has to end up on their back. Because I'm a dog like that. You can't back down from *anyone*, and you have to be ready to fight for a win, your teammates, and most importantly, the last name on your jersey. If you're a new player on a team and don't have a spot, you have to fight for one... figuratively and, in some cases, literally.

The Art of Controlled Aggression

There's a difference between playing wild and playing with purpose. The truly great ones understand this. When you step onto that field, you're not just an athlete; you're a predator. But here's the key: Predators don't waste energy. Every move has a purpose. Every step is calculated. Even the intensity itself is a weapon when wielded correctly.

Think about the great defensive players you've watched. Ray Lewis. Ronnie Lott. Troy Polamalu. These weren't just aggressive players; they were strategic warriors. They understood that true dominance comes from combining physical intensity with mental mastery.

This kind of controlled aggression isn't something you just turn on during game day. It's cultivated in practice, refined in training, and perfected through repetition. It's about building habits that make intensity your natural state when you step between those white lines.

The Psychology of Dominance

The shark tank mentality starts long before kickoff. It's in how you carry yourself in warm-ups. It's in your eyes when you line up across from your opponent. It's in the way you finish every single play, whether it's a touchdown or a routine block.

But here's what most people don't understand about true dominance: It's not about being the biggest, strongest, or fastest but about imposing your will. It's about making your opponent feel your presence in every single play. It's about breaking their spirit before you break their game plan.

When you're truly operating with a shark tank mentality, every snap is an opportunity to make a statement. Every block is a chance to establish dominance. Every route is a message to your opponent: You don't belong on the same field as me.

Building the Beast

You can't just flip a switch and become a shark. This mentality is built through thousands of repetitions in practice. It's forged in the weight room when you're pushing through that last set. It's developed during conditioning when your body is screaming to stop, but you keep pushing.

The beauty of this mindset is that it feeds on itself. Every extra rep, every additional sprint, and every bonus film session adds to your confidence. And when you step on that field knowing you've outworked everyone else, that's when the true shark tank mentality emerges.

Remember: On game day, there are no friends between those lines. There's no mercy. There's no taking plays off. There's just you, your brothers beside you, and a group of opponents who need to be reminded why they should have stayed home.

One of the biggest things for your development, in my opinion, is your work ethic. I could have started this book with this because if you're not willing to put in more work than the next man, if you're not comfortable being uncomfortable, or if you're not able to commit yourself to a physical test day in and day out, you probably won't make it past high school, to begin with. For perspective, under two percent of *all* high school players in the world are fortunate enough to earn a college scholarship. So, if you look at your current football roster, you'll be lucky if three of those guys get an opportunity to play at the college level.

The Uncomfortable Truth

Let's talk about something most people don't want to hear: Talent is overrated. Yes, you read that right. In fact, talent might be the most dangerous gift in football because it can make you lazy. It can make you think you can skip the hard work. It can make you believe you're special.

Football isn't a sport where you can rely on God-given talent alone. Wide receivers and DBs, specifically, depend on technique. Hours and hours of technical reps are needed to be an exceptional player.

Now that we have established this, let's dive into the offseason. If you're not doing everything you possibly can to get better, your path is going to be difficult.

The Price of Greatness

Think about this: While you're sleeping, someone else is training. While you're playing video games, someone else is studying film. While you're scrolling through social media, someone else is getting better. This isn't about guilt; it's about reality.

Training is where it starts. You have to *make time* to work on your craft. You need to be on the field, in the gym, dedicating time to perfecting your technique—whether it be your routes, speed, or backpedal. This commitment demands effort. If your body is trained to activate whenever you're doing something football-related, imagine how locked in you'll be during game time. The effort is crucial—100% every single rep. In summary, the only way to get better on the field is by actually doing it, not just thinking about it.

Your Second Home

The weight room should be your second home. Throughout your career, you'll realize just how beneficial it is. During the season, practice, training, and dedicating additional hours to your craft, along with reviewing game and practice film, should be a constant routine. Keep in mind that it's going to be tough. There will be days when you don't feel like going to the gym before practice or don't feel like stepping onto the field. Find something that motivates you. Understand that there's always someone out there working, so do everything you can not to be outworked.

The weight room isn't just about getting stronger; it's about building your armor. Every rep, every set, and every drop of sweat is an investment in your durability, explosiveness, and ability to dominate when it matters most. But it's also about something deeper: It's about proving to yourself, day after day, that you can push through barriers.

The No-Excuses Zone

Laziness is not an option if you really want it. You can't afford a day off playing video games all day. Stretch, hydrate, watch film—do something. The hours you put in don't lie. If you're not doing what you need to, you'll be exposed on the field. On the flip side, if you are doing the right things, it'll show. If nothing else, I hope you remember this chapter because this alone can catapult you into being a way better player.

Here's a truth that might hurt: Nobody cares about your excuses. Nobody cares that you're tired. Nobody cares that you're sore. Nobody cares that you had a bad day. The field doesn't care. Your opponents definitely don't. The only thing that matters is what you do with the time you have.

Remember: Extraordinary achievements require extraordinary effort. There's no shortcut to greatness. No elevator to success. You have to take the stairs, one grueling step at a time.

Learn to Set Goals

There's no better feeling than exceeding your expectations. Goals are one of the best ways to hold yourself accountable and stick to a routine. Goals keep you hungry for more, and in football, you must always want more. Complacency is not an option. There's always someone out there working for your spot. The higher up you go, the more you must stay motivated and consistent. Therefore, I always recommend setting goals because they keep you on an upward trajectory. When you have something to work toward, it's easier to stay motivated, even when you feel like you can dominate those around you.

Dreams vs. Goals

Let me tell you something about dreams: Everybody's got them. Every kid throwing a football in their backyard dreams of playing in the Super

Bowl. But dreams without deadlines are just wishes. Dreams without action plans are just fantasies. That's where goals come in.

Goals train your mind to sacrifice time and effort to achieve what needs to be accomplished. For instance, achieving a six-month goal requires consistent work. There will be times when you don't feel like it, but overcoming that adversity strengthens your mind. Thus, short-term, mid-term, and long-term goals should always be pursued and updated. Since this is Wide Receiver U, I have some homework for you guys.

Making It Real

1. *Grab a pen and paper.*

2. Write out three six-month goals in bold letters.

3. Think hard about them and take your time.

4. Focus on your weak areas, whether personal or sports-related.

5. Think of three things you want to achieve to become a better person.

6. Under each goal, list three actions you can take to achieve them. Don't cheat—this is important.

7. Tape it somewhere you'll see it every day (e.g., bathroom mirror, bedroom door, above your bed).

8. Seeing it daily will keep you reminded of the task at hand, and if you feel unmotivated, this will make you think twice about slacking off.

Why six months? Because it's long enough to achieve something significant but short enough to maintain urgency. It's the sweet spot between immediate gratification and long-term vision. Six months gives you enough time to transform a weakness into a strength, to turn a dream into reality.

The Complete Player

The goal is to become the best person you can be. Yes, *football player* falls under this category, but it's bigger than football. It starts in your head; this is how you become elite.

Think beyond just football goals. Want to improve your route-running? Great. But what about your GPA? Your leadership skills? Your character? The greatest players understand that excellence on the field is just one part of the equation. Every aspect of your life affects your performance.

The Final Push

Mindset is Step 1. If you're not committed to the journey and in love with the game, you won't make it to the next steps. At the end of the day, nobody will believe in you until you believe in yourself. If playing football at a high level is your goal, you must sell yourself and convince people—teams—why they should choose you over the next guy. You can't sell something you don't fully believe in, and you will undoubtedly face situations that require significant sacrifice and betting on yourself. I've done it countless times and proved myself right every single time.

You're about to embark on a journey that will test everything you've got. Your physical strength, your mental toughness, your emotional resilience, all of it will be challenged. But remember that every great player started exactly where you are right now. With a dream, a pen, some paper, and the courage to write down goals that scared them.

Now, it's your turn. What are you going to write on that paper? More importantly, what are you going to do about it?

Building Your Mental Toolkit

Every elite athlete knows something that average players don't: The game is won long before you step onto the field. While physical preparation is crucial, it's your mental toolkit that often makes the difference between good and great, clutch and choke, and victory and defeat.

Think about the moments before a big game. Your heart's racing. The butterflies are doing backflips in your stomach. Everyone feels this, even the pros. But the great ones? They've trained their minds to transform that nervous energy into rocket fuel for performance.

The Power of Visualization

Here's something I learned early that changed my game forever: Your brain can't tell the difference between a vividly imagined experience and a real one. When you visualize catching that game-winning touchdown, running that perfect route, or making that crucial block, your neurons are firing in the exact same pattern as if you were actually doing it. The science behind this is fascinating: Studies have shown that athletes who combine physical practice with visualization improve faster than those who only practice physically (*How Athletes Use Visualization to Enhance Performance*, 2024).

Think about that for a second. Every time you vividly imagine performing a perfect route, your brain is laying down the same neural pathways as if you were actually running it. You're literally programming your nervous system for success, training your body while lying in bed.

But this isn't about just daydreaming. This is about deliberate mental practice. When I visualize a route, I feel the grass under my cleats. I see the defender's stance. I feel the burst off the line. I experience the head fake, the hip switch, and the break. I see the ball spinning toward me. I feel it hit my hands. Every detail, every sensation, and every movement is there in vivid Technicolor.

Let me break down exactly how I use this before a big game. The night before, I'll find a quiet spot. Maybe in my hotel room, maybe in a quiet corner of the facility. I close my eyes and start with my first expected play. I see the defensive coverage we're expecting. I feel my pre-snap routine—the way I adjust my gloves, the three deep breaths I take, and the way I settle into my stance.

Then, I run the play in my mind. Not just the ideal version but every possible variation. What if the corner plays press? What if they're in zone? What if I need to adjust my route? I visualize every scenario, my response to each, and the feeling of success in every situation.

But here's the key: I also visualize adversity. I see myself getting jammed at the line. I feel the frustration. Then, I see myself fighting through it, maintaining perfect technique, and making the play anyway. Because visualization isn't just about seeing success; it's about preparing for every possibility.

Start doing this before practice. Before your workouts. Before you go to sleep at night. The more you practice visualization, the more natural it becomes and the more powerful its effects are. Start small, maybe just one play, one route, one situation. But make it detailed. Make it real. Feel every step, every cut, every catch.

I remember a game where this paid off hugely. Fourth quarter, game on the line, and the defense showed a coverage we hadn't seen on film. But I had visualized similar scenarios so many times that my body knew exactly what to adjust without my mind having to think about it. The route changed, but the result was the same: touchdown. That's the power of visualization.

Make it part of your daily routine. When you're in the weight room, visualize how each rep is making you stronger for game day. When you're studying film, don't just watch: Imagine yourself exploiting what you're seeing. When working on your routes, see yourself using these patterns to break open in crucial moments.

Some might be thinking this sounds like make-believe. Like kids playing pretend. But let me tell you: Every elite athlete I know does this in some form. The greats understand that the game is won, as previously mentioned, long before they step on the field, and much of that victory happens in their minds.

The beauty of visualization is that you can do it anywhere, anytime. Stuck in traffic? Visualize your routes. Waiting in line? See yourself making plays. Every moment becomes an opportunity to improve, to program your mind and body for success.

Remember: Your body can only do what your mind has prepared it to do. Start training both, and watch how quickly your game transforms.

Game-Day Mental Preparation

Your pregame routine isn't just about getting your body ready; it's about preparing your mind for battle. Therefore, create a routine that gets you in the zone. Maybe it's certain music. Maybe it's going through your plays in your head. Maybe it's quiet time to focus and center yourself. Whatever it is, make it consistent. Make it yours.

Think of it like programming a computer. Each part of your routine is a line of code telling your mind and body, "It's time to go to work." Over time, these triggers become automatic. The moment you start your routine, your mind begins shifting into game mode.

Focus: Your Secret Weapon

Let's talk about focus—real focus. Not the kind where you're sort of paying attention, but the kind where the rest of the world disappears, and there's nothing but you and your assignment. This kind of focus is like a superpower, but it needs to be trained.

Start in practice. When you're running drills, don't just go through the motions. Be present for every rep. Feel every step. Analyze every movement. The more you practice this laser focus in training, the more natural it becomes in games.

But here's the real secret: Focus isn't about never getting distracted; it's about how quickly you can refocus when distractions emerge. Because they will emerge. The crowd will be screaming. The defense will be talking. You might be tired, hurting, or frustrated. Your ability to snap back into focus when it matters most? That's what separates the good from the great.

Building Mental Endurance

Just like your body needs conditioning, your mind needs endurance training. This means pushing through when your brain is screaming to stop. It means maintaining technique when you're exhausted. It means executing plays perfectly in the fourth quarter when your body's running on empty.

Start building this endurance in practice. When you're tired and want to slow down, that's exactly when you need to dial in your focus even more. Make your practice conditions tougher than game conditions. Add extra challenges to your drills. Force yourself to think and perform under stress.

Remember: Mental toughness isn't about being tough all the time. It's about being tough when it matters. It's about making the crucial catch when your hands are burning. It's about running the perfect route when your legs feel like lead. It's about maintaining your technique when everything in your body is telling you to slack off.

Your mental toolkit isn't something you're born with; it's something you build, day by day, rep by rep. Every time you push through fatigue, every time you maintain focus when it would be easier to check out, and every time you execute despite distractions, you're adding another tool to your kit.

Moreover, the beautiful thing about mental training is that it compounds gradually. Hence, each small victory builds confidence. Each moment of focused practice strengthens your concentration. Each visualization session sharpens your mental game. Over time, these small improvements add up to something remarkable: an unshakeable mental foundation that will carry you through any challenge the game throws your way.

Take these tools seriously. Practice them with the same dedication you bring to your physical training because when the game is on the line, when the pressure is mounting, and when everything is at stake, it's not just your body that needs to be ready. It's your mind that will make the difference.

The Champion's Mindset in Action

Let me tell you about a moment that changed everything for me.

It was my first NFL training camp with the Bengals. I'm lining up against guys I used to watch on TV, guys with Pro Bowl appearances, guys with Super Bowl rings. And for a split second, I let that get to me. I started thinking, *Man, these are the guys.* That split second of doubt showed up in my routes: My cuts weren't as sharp, and my breaks weren't as decisive.

Then, one of the veteran receivers pulled me aside. He said something I'll never forget: "Hey, rookie, you're not here by accident. You didn't fly to Canada just to be nice. You're here because you belong here. Now play like it."

That's when it hit me: The champion's mindset isn't about being fearless. It's about being afraid and doing it anyway. It's about understanding that doubt is normal but letting it fuel you instead of stopping you.

Learning From the Greats

When you study the game's legends, you start to notice something: Their greatest achievements weren't just physical; they were mental. Let's dig deeper into what made these athletes truly exceptional.

Jerry Rice

Jerry Rice's hill wasn't just any hill. It was a 2.5-mi monster that broke anyone who tried to run with him. Teammates, opponents, and even other pro athletes would come to train with him. Almost none could finish. But here's what made Rice different: He didn't just run that hill; he sprinted it. In the scorching California heat, when others were resting, Rice was pushing himself to the absolute limit.

But why? Because Rice understood something fundamental about greatness: It's built in these moments when nobody's watching. Every step up that hill was a deposit in his confidence bank. Every workout was adding to his psychological armor. By the time he stepped onto the field, he had already won the mental battle. His opponents might have been just as talented, but none of them had run that hill. None of them had paid the price he had paid.

Think about that for a moment. The greatest receiver in NFL history wasn't content with being great. He was obsessed with widening the gap between himself and everyone else. Even after breaking every record, even after the Super Bowl rings, even after the Hall of Fame was a certainty, he kept running that hill.

Tom Brady

Then, there's Tom Brady. The 199th pick. The guy "too slow" to be a star. The backup who wasn't supposed to be anything more than a clipboard holder. But Brady had something that talent alone can't give you: an unshakeable belief in himself combined with a burning desire to prove everyone wrong.

Even after winning his first Super Bowl, Brady kept the scouting reports that criticized him. He kept the list of quarterbacks drafted before him. Six rings later, he still practiced like he was fighting for a roster spot. That's not just motivation; that's a mindset. A mindset that says your past achievements don't guarantee future success. A mindset that understands greatness isn't a destination but a daily choice.

When Champions Fail

Here's something they don't show you on ESPN's highlights: Michael Jordan missed over 9,000 shots in his career. Rice dropped passes. Brady threw interceptions. But what sets champions apart isn't their ability to avoid failure; it's their response to it.

That playoff game I mentioned? Let me paint the full picture. Fourth quarter, game on the line, perfect pass right to my hands... and I dropped it. At that moment, it felt like the world stopped. You could hear the collective groan from the crowd. The sideline went quiet. In my head, all I could hear was every doubt, every criticism, and every person who said I couldn't make it.

But champions don't stay in that moment. They use it. The next morning, while most players were still sleeping off the loss, I was on that field. The sun wasn't even up yet. I set up the JUGS machine to throw that exact same pass. Over and over and over. Fifty catches weren't enough. A hundred weren't enough. I needed to turn that failure into an impossibility in my mind.

By the time I was done, my hands were burning. My legs were shaking. But something had changed in my mind. That drop didn't own me anymore. I owned it. I had turned it into a strength. The next time that play came up, there wasn't a doubt in my mind. I knew I would make the catch because I had already made it a thousand times in my redemption session.

That's the difference between good players and great ones. Good players try to forget their failures. Great ones use them as building blocks. Every mistake becomes a lesson. Every setback becomes a setup. Every failure becomes fuel.

Remember this: The path to greatness isn't a straight line. It's a series of failures, setbacks, and moments that test your resolve. The question isn't whether these moments will come—they will. The question is: What will you do when they do? Will you let them break you, or will you let them make you?

The choice, as always, is yours.

Your Daily Championship Practice

The champion's mindset isn't something you put on like a uniform before the game. It's something you build, day by day, through consistent habits and routines.

Start with your morning. Champions own their mornings. Before you check your phone, before you do anything else, take five minutes to visualize your goals. See yourself making plays. Feel the success. Make it real in your mind before you make it real on the field.

During practice, hold yourself to a championship standard. No lazy reps. No half-speed routes. No *good enough*. If you're not proud of a rep, do it again. And again. Until it's perfect.

After practice, while everyone else is heading home, stay for extra work. But be smart about it. Quality over quantity. Focus on one specific thing you want to improve and make every extra rep count.

Building Unshakeable Mental Toughness

Mental toughness isn't about being tough all the time. It's about being tough when it matters. It's about executing when you're tired, focusing when you're distracted, and having confidence when you're doubting.

Here's how you build it: Put yourself in uncomfortable situations deliberately. If you're a receiver, practice with weighted gloves. If you're a DB, practice with restricted vision. Make your practice harder than any game could ever be.

Challenge yourself daily. Set small, achievable goals for each practice. Then, crush them. Then, set new ones. Keep pushing that ceiling higher.

Most importantly, remember this: The champion's mindset isn't about being special. It's about doing special things consistently. It's about the daily decisions that nobody sees but everyone feels on game day.

Every time you choose the hard way over the easy way, you're building that mindset. Every time you push through when others would quit, you're strengthening it. Every time you maintain your standards when others lower theirs, you're proving it.

The champion's mindset isn't just about what you do; it's about who you become in the process. It's about transforming yourself into someone who doesn't just dream about success but expects it, works for it, and lives it.

Remember: Champions aren't born. They're built, decision by decision, day by day, rep by rep. The question isn't whether you can become one. The question is: Are you willing to do what it takes?

Your Next Steps

Let's take everything we've covered in this chapter and turn it into action. Right now, before you move forward, you need to commit these fundamental truths to memory:

- The mindset of a champion isn't a gift; it's a choice you make every single day. Every morning, when you wake up, you're either getting better or getting worse. There's no standing still in this game.

- Your mental preparation is just as important as your physical one. Maybe more. Because when the game is on the line, when you're tired, when everything is stacked against you, it's your mind that will carry you through.

- Success leaves clues. The greats we talked about—Jerry Rice and Tom Brady—didn't just happen to be great. They built their greatness through daily habits, unwavering commitment, and a mindset that refused to settle for anything less than excellence.

Your Action Items

Before you move on to the next chapter, I need you to do these things:

- Take out that paper right now and write down your three six-month goals. Not tomorrow, not later—now.

- Create your visualization routine. Start with five minutes every morning and every night.

- Begin your mental training log. Track your mindset wins and challenges daily.

- Identify your mental triggers, both positive and negative. What builds your confidence? What shakes it?

The Academic Connection

Now, you might be wondering why our next chapter focuses on academic performance. Here's why: The same mindset that makes you great on the field will make you great in the classroom. That laser focus you use to learn plays? Use it to master your subjects. That discipline that gets you to early morning workouts? Apply it to your study schedule.

Because here's the truth: Being a complete athlete means being a complete person. The dedication it takes to master a playbook is the same dedication it takes to master a textbook. The attention to detail that makes you great at running routes will make you great at solving problems.

Remember: Every NFL team looks at your academic performance. They want to know if you can learn, focus, and commit to excellence in all areas of your life. Your GPA isn't just a number; it's a testament to your character.

As we move into Chapter 2, keep this mindset we've built. The field and the classroom aren't separate worlds; they're both arenas where champions are made. The only difference is the uniform you wear.

So, are you ready to take this champion's mindset into every aspect of your life? Turn the page, and let's get to work.

Remember: The mind is where every battle is won or lost. Master your mind, and you'll master your game.

Let's go.

Chapter 2:
Grades Matter

Let me tell you something that might hurt: Right now, there's a kid with your same dream, same position, and same level of talent, but better grades. And guess what? He's going to get opportunities you won't. That's not fair, right? Welcome to the real world of football, where talent alone doesn't open doors.

Do you think I'm exaggerating? I've seen five-star recruits get passed over because they couldn't maintain the minimum GPA. I've watched Division I dreams turn into Division II realities because someone thought their athletic ability would excuse their academic laziness. I've seen NFL-caliber talent waste away because they couldn't stay eligible.

This chapter isn't going to be comfortable. We're going to talk about the part of football that nobody likes to discuss, the part that happens in classrooms, not weight rooms. The part that requires you to be as disciplined with your textbooks as you are with your playbook.

Because here's the truth that nobody tells you when they're hyping up your athletic potential: Your grades aren't just numbers. They're keys. Keys that unlock doors to better programs, better opportunities, and better futures. And once those doors close because of poor academics, no amount of touchdowns, no highlight reels, and no combine performances can open them back up.

Do you want to know how I know? Because I lived it. I made the mistakes. I learned the hard way that being a student-athlete means being a student first. And I'm about to share every painful lesson with you so you don't have to learn them the same way I did.

Are you ready for some uncomfortable truths? Good. Let's talk about what it really means to be a student-athlete.

The Student in Student-Athlete

Notice how they put *student* first in *student-athlete*? That's not an accident. It's not just some fancy term colleges made up. It's a reality check written right there in plain English: Before you're an athlete, you're a student. And there's a reason for that order.

Here's what they don't tell you at those football camps and combines: Out of roughly 1.1 million high school football players, only about 73,000 will play college football. That's already a tiny percentage. But here's the real kicker: Nearly 40% of those spots go unfilled not because of a lack of talent but because of academic ineligibility.

Think about that. Kids with the speed, strength, and skill to play at the next level watch their dreams slip away because they thought their talent would save them. They bought into the biggest lie in sports: that being good enough on the field makes you immune to what happens in the classroom.

"But what about the five-star recruits?" you might ask. "What about the guys everyone wants?" Let me tell you something about those top programs you dream of playing for. Alabama, Ohio State, Clemson... they're not just looking for athletes. They're looking for complete packages. Because when you have your pick of the best athletes in the country, guess what becomes the difference-maker? Grades. Character. Reliability.

You see, your GPA tells coaches more than just how well you do in class. It answers the following questions:

- Can you handle complex playbooks?
- Will you be eligible when they need you?
- Can you manage your time?
- Do you take care of business without someone standing over you?
- Are you disciplined enough to do the things you don't want to do?

Every time you slack off in class, every assignment you blow off, and every test you don't study for, you're not just hurting your GPA; you're sending a message to every college coach out there: "I'm not reliable. I take shortcuts. I don't finish what I start."

I learned this lesson the hard way. I thought my talent would be enough. I thought being a 6'5" receiver with good hands and speed would open all the doors I needed. Man, was I wrong. And I'm about to tell you exactly how that worked out for me—or didn't work out, to be more precise.

Let me tell you a story about a kid who had all the physical tools, who could dominate on Friday nights, who had college scouts drooling over his potential. A kid who learned, painfully and publicly, that talent without academics is like a Ferrari without gas—looks great, but ain't going nowhere.

That kid was me. And trust me, you don't want to learn this lesson the way I did.

A Hard Lesson Learned

High school and college are some of the most important phases in your journey. They set the foundation for everything that follows. The sooner you understand the importance of the little things, the easier your path will be. I know a lot of you don't want to hear this, but I have to stress the importance of keeping your grades up and genuinely trying in class. This is part of being an athlete; there is no athlete without the student part.

In high school, I was the kind of kid who didn't do anything I didn't want to. I didn't enjoy learning about history or math; all I wanted to do was play football. I wasn't dumb, but I just didn't try. Honestly, I believed that because I was so good at football, I would get an opportunity to play at a university just because of that.

I'll never forget one moment during my senior season. We were deep in the playoffs, playing against our rivals. I had an absolute monster game with three touchdowns and a pick on defense, and we barely came out of the game with a win. After the game, I was talking with my dad when a man approached us wearing a University of Montana hat. He told me I had a great game and was impressed. He expressed his school's interest in me and asked me to send him my transcripts to further the recruiting process. Communication was steady until they received my transcripts. Long story short, I never heard back from him.

The Reality Check

Let me paint this picture even clearer for you. Imagine being on top of the world. You just had the game of your life. Three touchdowns. A pick on defense. The kind of performance that gets you noticed, that makes scouts sit up in their seats. And there he was, a Division I recruiter, right there, interested in you. The dream is happening. This is your moment.

Then silence. Complete silence. All because of some numbers on a piece of paper that had nothing to do with your athletic ability.

My grades weren't terrible—probably around a 2.0 at that time—but I realized it was too late to raise my GPA. From what I understood, word spread to other schools in Canada that my grades were low, resulting in *zero* offers by February after the season, even as a 6'5" receiver. I could write pages about how hard I tried to improve my grades, but I'll spare you the details. Just know my school schedule was packed with honors classes and two math courses to make up for previous years. Needless to say, I was nervous, but I still had hope.

The Painful Truth

Do you know what's worse than not getting recruited? Knowing you did it to yourself. Every "C" I got because I didn't study, every assignment I blew off because I thought football was more important, they all came back to haunt me. And here's the thing about grades: Unlike a bad play or a tough loss, you can't make up for them with one good performance. They follow you. They add up, and by the time you realize how much they matter, it's often too late to fix them.

Think about this: I was a 6'5" receiver with proven playmaking ability. That's the kind of physical profile that scouts are looking for. But it wasn't enough. All that God-given talent, all those hours in the weight room, all those extra reps after practice, none of it mattered because I hadn't handled my business in the classroom.

This isn't just my story. This is happening right now all across the country. Athletes with NFL potential are watching their dreams fade away, not because they can't play, but because they didn't take care of the student part of student-athlete.

The Real World of Athletic Recruitment

Let's pull back the curtain on how college recruitment really works. Not the highlight reels and social media hype but the cold, hard process that determines your future.

Here's what happens when a college gets interested in you: The first thing they look at? Not your game film. Not your stats. They check your core GPA and test scores. Why? Because if you don't meet the minimum academic requirements, everything else is irrelevant. Division I schools require a minimum 2.3 GPA in core courses. Division II needs a 2.2. These aren't suggestions; they're hard lines that even Nick Saban can't override.

But here's the real secret: These are just minimums. In reality, most top programs are looking for much higher GPAs. Why? Because they're not just recruiting athletes; they're managing risk. Every scholarship is a six-figure investment by the school, so they need to know you'll stay eligible, handle the academic workload, and represent their program well.

Think about it from a coach's perspective. You have two recruits:

- Player A: amazing athlete, 2.4 GPA

- Player B: similarly talented, 3.5 GPA

Who's the safer bet? Who's less likely to become academically ineligible mid-season? Who's more likely to handle college-level coursework while learning a complex playbook?

This isn't just about getting in; it's about staying in. College football is a full-time job on top of being a full-time student. You'll have early morning workouts, film sessions, practice, travel, and games, all while maintaining your grades. The academic demands are intense: study halls, progress reports, and mandatory tutoring sessions. If you couldn't handle high school coursework, how would you manage this?

Let me break down what recruiters are really evaluating when they look at your academic record:

- Reliability: Can they count on you to handle your business without constant supervision?

- Time management: Your grades show whether you can balance multiple responsibilities, a crucial skill for college athletes.

- Learning capacity: How quickly can you absorb new information? This matters as much for complex playbooks as it does for classroom material.

- Character: Your academic record reflects your work ethic, discipline, and response to challenges.

Here's another reality check: The competition is fierce. For every spot on a college roster, there are dozens of qualified athletes. When programs are choosing between similarly talented players, academics become the tiebreaker. A solid GPA doesn't just show you're smart; it shows you're serious.

Do you want some numbers? Division I programs have about 85 scholarships to give, but they might be recruiting 200–300 players for those spots. If they have to eliminate half of those prospects based on academics alone, which side of that cut do you want to be on?

And let's talk about academic scholarships. Strong grades don't just keep you eligible; they can help pay for school. Many athletes combine athletic and academic scholarships, taking pressure off both themselves and the program. This makes you an even more attractive recruit.

The harsh truth? Your 40-yard dash time might get you noticed, but your transcript is what gets you recruited. Your highlight reel might get them excited, but your GPA determines if they can take you seriously.

Remember: Colleges aren't just recruiting players for next season; they're recruiting graduates for the next four years. Subsequently, they need to know you can handle the full journey, not just the first step.

This isn't about being a genius. It's about showing you can handle your business. It's about proving you're worth the investment. Because at the end of the day, that's what a scholarship is: an investment in your future, both on and off the field.

Making Choices That Matter

In the end, I received two offers: from the University of Saskatchewan—which wasn't very strong at the time—and the University of Calgary, the number two-ranked team in the country. Wasn't that something? God works in mysterious ways, and I could see it was a blessing to test where my head was. Saskatchewan was offering a starting spot, while Calgary said there was a spot up for grabs, but I'd have to compete for it. I made that decision quickly and was ready to work and bet on myself. I could have taken the easy route by committing to a less competitive team for playing time, but I've always preferred to earn what I have. Plus, being on a stronger team would push me to improve as an individual through competition.

The Choices That Define Us

That decision I made between Saskatchewan and Calgary? It wasn't just about football. It was about character. About who I wanted to be.

Sometimes, life hands you a choice that looks like it's about one thing, but it's really about everything.

Think about it: Saskatchewan was offering certainty. A starting spot. The easy path. Calgary was offering nothing but an opportunity to compete. No guarantees. No promises. Just a chance to prove myself against the best.

This is the same choice you face every day in your academic life. Do you take the easy classes to protect your GPA? Or do you challenge yourself with honors courses that might make you struggle but will make you stronger? Do you coast through with minimum effort or push yourself to excel?

The Character Test

Your academic choices reflect more than just your study habits; they reveal the core of who you are. Every decision you make speaks volumes about your character:

- When you choose to study while others are out having fun, you're prioritizing your future over fleeting pleasures.

- When you seek help instead of giving up, you show resilience and humility, valuing growth over pride.

- When you challenge yourself with demanding courses rather than settling for easy A's, you embrace the mindset of continuous improvement.

- When you stay after class to master a concept, you reveal a hunger for understanding that goes beyond mere grades.

- When you choose the harder right over the easier wrong, you demonstrate integrity and courage in the face of difficult decisions.

These actions aren't just about academics; they're about who you are becoming. They reveal your drive, priorities, and commitment to excellence in every facet of life. In these moments, you're not just building your future; you're shaping your character.

Beyond the Classroom

The way you approach your academics is a reflection of how you'll approach everything else in life. Consider this:

- The discipline it takes to study when you don't feel like it is the same discipline you'll rely on for early-morning workouts or late-night practices.

- The humility to ask for help when you're stuck in class is the same humility you'll need to learn from experienced coaches and seasoned teammates.

- The resilience to bounce back from a disappointing grade mirrors the resilience you'll need to recover after a tough loss or setback on the field.

When coaches review your academic record, they're not just evaluating numbers on a page:

- They're seeing patterns in how you handle responsibility.

- They're noticing the choices you've made under pressure.

- Most importantly, they're gaining insight into your character—the very foundation of how you'll show up in life and competition.

The Growth Mindset

Choosing the harder path—whether it's stepping into the arena to compete for a coveted spot at Calgary or enrolling in a course that pushes you beyond your comfort zone—speaks volumes about your mindset. It's a bold declaration that you're not afraid to risk failure. You're not looking for shortcuts, nor are you chasing guarantees. Instead, you're chasing improvement, constantly seeking to elevate yourself to new heights.

This growth mindset is the dividing line between good athletes and great ones. Good athletes work hard and stay consistent, but great athletes embrace the discomfort of challenge. They lean into adversity, understanding that comfort is the enemy of growth. For them, challenges aren't obstacles; they're opportunities to refine their skills, test their limits, and rise above the competition.

In this setting, struggles, far from being something to avoid, are seen as the very foundation of strength. Each stumble and every difficult moment becomes a stepping stone toward excellence. And competition? It's not something to fear but something to welcome. It's the crucible that sharpens their abilities, the proving ground that pushes them to be better than they were yesterday.

By choosing the harder right over the easier wrong, you're showing the world—and yourself that you're ready to commit to greatness. This mindset, this refusal to settle for mediocrity, is what transforms potential into achievement and dreams into reality. It's not just about being better today: it's about striving to be extraordinary every day.

Making Your Own Choices

Now, you're facing your own choices. *Maybe it's between the following:*

- taking that AP class or settling for regular courses

- joining that study group or trying to coast by

- asking for help or pretending you understand

- doing the extra credit or settling for *good enough*

Remember: These choices aren't just about grades. They're about who you're becoming. They're about the kind of athlete, student, and person you want to be.

When I chose Calgary over Saskatchewan, I wasn't just choosing a school. I was choosing a path. I was choosing growth over comfort. Challenge over certainty. The harder right over the easier wrong.

What will you choose?

When Talent Isn't Enough

Fast forward 3 years to the offseason after my 3rd season at Calgary. I was a 20-year-old, 3-year starter since my freshman year heading into the offseason. My first 2 seasons were decent: I was the 3rd or 4th option on a team full of veterans, putting up 300–500 yd each season while also serving as a returner, making a name for myself as a game-changing player. My 3rd year was my breakout season: 1,008 yd in 8 games, the top receiver in the country by far. But I was coming off an academic probation year for not taking my classes seriously and foolishly believing my talent alone would get me to the league.

That February, I was kicked out of school for low grades and became ineligible to play in what would have been my draft year of college football. I know. I was mad at myself, too. One more season, even remotely close to the last one, and I likely would have been drafted late in the NFL draft as a kid from Canada. I still made it happen, but it could have gone much better than it did.

The Price of Academic Neglect

Let that sink in for a moment. Top receiver in the country. NFL potential. Everything going right on the field. And then, gone. Not because of an injury. Not because of a lack of talent. But because I couldn't handle my business in the classroom.

This isn't just my story. I've seen it happen over and over:
- the five-star recruit who never made it to campus because he couldn't qualify
- the all-conference player who lost his eligibility mid-season
- the draft prospect who watched his stock plummet because teams questioned his ability to learn complex NFL systems

The Narrow Window

Here's what nobody tells you about football: Your window of opportunity is incredibly small. Most players get one shot, one chance to make their mark. And that window? It's not just about staying healthy or performing on the field. It's about staying eligible.

Think about my situation. I had everything lined up:
- Physical tools? Check.
- Game production? Check.
- NFL interest? Check.
- Draft year momentum? Check.

But none of it mattered because I couldn't stay in school. That's how fragile this dream is. That's how quickly it can slip away.

The Real Cost

When you neglect your academics, you're not just risking your eligibility. You're

- limiting your options for colleges.
- reducing your scholarship opportunities.
- putting your team at risk.
- damaging your reputation with coaches and scouts.
- closing doors before they even open.

And here's the worst part: Unlike a physical injury, academic neglect is entirely preventable. It's a self-inflicted wound. A choice you make every time you decide not to study, not to attend class, or not to do the work.

Beyond Football

But let's talk about something even more important than missed opportunities on the field: What happens when the game ends? Whether after high school, college, or even the NFL, every playing career eventually comes to a close. Then what?

That's where your academic record takes center stage. It's not just a collection of grades; it's a blueprint of your dedication and preparation for life after football. A poor academic record can:

- limit your job opportunities, making it harder to compete in a professional world that values discipline and effort.
- reduce your earning potential, leaving you with fewer options to build the life you've envisioned.
- close doors to graduate school or further education that could expand your career horizons.
- impact your ability to transition into coaching, sports management, or other football-related careers that often require a solid educational foundation.

Football may open doors, but your academics keep them open. The choices you make now, on and off the field, will shape the opportunities available to you when the game is over. Playing football is temporary, but the habits, discipline, and achievements you build in the classroom are permanent. They're what prepare you to win—not just in the game, but in life.

The Reality Check

Here's a harsh truth: The NFL doesn't care how hard your classes were. They don't care if you have struggled with math or hated writing papers. They care about results. They care about reliability. They care about whether you can be trusted to handle your business professionally.

When teams look at academic issues, they see red flags:

- Can this player learn our system?
- Will he be professional and responsible?
- Can he handle complex assignments?
- Is he mature enough for the NFL?

Breaking the Cycle

The good news? You can break this cycle. Right now. Today. It's never too early to start taking academics seriously, but it can quickly become too late.

Remember: Talent might get you noticed, but character and competence keep you in the game. Don't let academic neglect be the reason your dreams die. Don't let my story become your story.

Building Academic Success

Let's get practical. You know grades matter. You know talent isn't enough. Now, let's talk about how to actually make it happen because saying "study harder" isn't enough; you need a game plan for academics just like you have one for football. And here's the thing: The systems I'm about to teach you? They'll serve you well beyond your playing days.

Time Management: Your Most Valuable Life Skill

Think about your day like a playbook. Every hour is a play call, and how you execute determines your success. This isn't just about football or school; this is about building habits that will serve you in any career, challenge, or goal you pursue.

The Power Block System

Break your day into blocks, just like a pro:

- morning power hours (6–8 a.m.): workouts–film study
- class time (8–2 p.m.): full focus, no distractions
- practice–team time (2–6 p.m.): football focus
- evening study block (7–9 p.m.): academic grind
- recovery–prep time (9–10 p.m.): next day setup

Here's what Fortune 500 CEOs, successful entrepreneurs, and high achievers across every field understand: Structure creates freedom. When you master time management in college, you're not just learning how to balance football and academics; you're learning how to balance multiple priorities, handle pressure, and execute at a high level across different areas of life.

Making Every Minute Count

Road games aren't excuses for falling behind. They're opportunities to master the art of productivity in any situation:

- bus rides: perfect for flashcards and review
- hotel time: quiet study space without distractions
- team meals: group study with teammates in your classes
- flight time: deep focus work with no Internet distractions

This skill translates directly to professional life. Whether you end up in the NFL, running a business, or leading in any field, you'll need to maximize every minute. Top performers in any industry know how to turn *dead time* into productive time.

Study Skills That Score in Life

Just like you need proper technique on the field, you need proper technique in your studies. These aren't just academic skills; they're life skills.

The Focus Formation

Set up your study space like you set up for a play:
- clear workspace—like a clear mind pre-snap
- all materials ready—like having your equipment checked
- phone on *Do Not Disturb*—no defensive distractions
- water and snacks prepped—maintaining your energy

This same approach works in any professional setting. The ability to create an environment conducive to focus and productivity is invaluable in any career.

The Note-Taking Playbook

Take notes like you study film because, in life, details matter. Think about it: When you're breaking down game film, you don't just watch it once and hope you remember everything. You study it. You break it down. You look for patterns. You make notes about what works and what doesn't. Your class notes should get the same treatment.

Breaking Down the Game Plan

Think of your notes like a football playbook. Your main concepts are like your offensive schemes: They're your foundation, your go-to plays.

Write them down clearly and boldly, where you can find them fast. Make them stand out like they would on a play card.

The supporting details? They're like individual player assignments on each play. Just as every player has a specific job that makes the whole play work, these details, examples, and explanations make the main ideas come to life. Write them underneath each main concept, showing how everything connects to the bigger picture.

Those questions you write in the margins? Think of them like adjustment calls. Just as you need to adjust plays based on what the defense shows, you need to mark things you don't understand and note where you need to dig deeper. These are your *what-if* scenarios that need answers.

And reviewing your notes? That's your film study. Just like how you watch the game film multiple times to catch everything, go back through your notes the same day you take them. Clean them up, make them clearer, and fill in gaps while the information is fresh. Look for patterns and connections, just like you do when studying an opponent.

Preparation Principles

Whether it's a test, game, or business presentation, preparation follows the same rules:

1. Start early—no cramming.

2. Practice under real conditions.

3. Know what you're up against.

4. Have multiple strategies ready.

5. Build confidence through thorough preparation.

Building Your Success Network

Success in any field is about relationships and resources. Learn to build and use your network.

Authority Figure Relationships

Whether it's professors now or bosses later:

- Make early connections.
- Show up prepared.
- Engage actively.
- Communicate proactively.
- Handle responsibilities professionally.

Support System Utilization

In football, academics, or life, note the following:

- Advisors are your strategic planners.
- Mentors are your experienced guides.
- Peer groups are your collaboration network.
- Specialists are your expert resources.

The Champion's Daily Routine

Build habits that translate to any field.

Morning Excellence

- Review daily objectives.
- Check upcoming commitments.
- Prepare necessary materials.
- Review previous work–notes.
- Set specific daily goals.

Peak Performance Time

- Arrive early.

- Position yourself for success.
- Engage actively.
- Ask quality questions.
- Document important points.
- Take initiative.

Evening Mastery

- Review the day's learning.
- Prepare for tomorrow.
- Maintain organized systems.
- Utilize team resources.
- Plan ahead.

The Extra Mile: Excellence in Everything

The same mindset that makes you do extra reps after practice should apply to everything you pursue:

- Go beyond minimum requirements.
- Start early on all tasks.
- Study the successful.
- Build collaborative networks.
- Use downtime productively.

Remember: These aren't just academic strategies; they're success principles. The same discipline that makes you great in football and academics will make you exceptional in life. Every class is a preparation for future challenges. Every assignment is a chance to build professional habits. Every test is an opportunity to prove your ability to perform under pressure.

The real secret? Success leaves clues. The habits that make you a better student-athlete are the same habits that make you successful in any field. Time management, focused preparation, relationship building, and consistent execution are universal success principles.

Don't just survive academically; build habits of excellence that will serve you for life because whether you're on the field, in the classroom, or in your future career, excellence is a choice you make every day.

Resources at Your Disposal

Let me tell you something about successful athletes: They're not just hard workers but smart workers. They know when to ask for help, how to use every resource available, and how to maximize every advantage they can get. Think of it like having a full coaching staff for your academics.

Your Academic Support Team

Just like you have position coaches, strength coaches, and coordinators for football, you have an entire support system ready to help you succeed academically. Here's how to use them:

Academic Advisors: Your Academic Coordinators

These are your game planners for academic success. They know
- which classes fit your schedule.

- how to maintain eligibility.
- when to take challenging courses.
- how to balance your academic load.

Meet with them regularly, not just when you're in trouble. They can spot potential problems before they become disasters, just like a good coordinator sees weaknesses before they're exploited.

Tutoring Services: Your Position Coaches

Every school offers free tutoring. Use it. Not just when you're struggling, but to excel. Think about it: You wouldn't wait until you're playing terribly to work with your position coach, would you? The same principle applies here.

A good tutor can:
- break down complex concepts
- help you develop better study strategies
- identify your weak spots
- give you extra practice on difficult material

Study Groups: Your Practice Squad

Find your academic teammates. Look for:
- other athletes who understand your schedule
- strong students who raise the bar
- classmates who complement your strengths
- people who take it as seriously as you do

Just like in football, you rise to the level of your competition. Hence, surround yourself with academic excellence.

The Technology Playbook

In today's world, you have more tools at your disposal than ever before. Here are the apps we recommend at the time of writing this book. As tech evolves, you might find better options. Use whatever works best for you.

Study Apps That Score

These are like your film room for academics:
- Quizlet: For flashcards and quick review.
- Khan Academy: Free tutoring in multiple subjects.
- Grammarly: Your offensive line for writing assignments.
- Photomath: Step-by-step math solutions.

- Notion or Evernote: Your digital playbook for notes.

Organization Tools: Your Academic Equipment

Just like you maintain your football gear, maintain your academic organization:
- Google Calendar: Schedule everything.
- Microsoft OneNote: Digital note-taking.
- Todoist: Task management.
- Forest App: Stay focused during study time.
- Google Drive: Keep all your work backed up and accessible.

Time Management Tech

These tools help you make the most of every minute:
- Focus@Will: Background music for studying.
- Focus Timer: Break study sessions into manageable chunks.
- RescueTime: Track how you're really spending your time.
- Any.do: Manage tasks and reminders.

Making It All Work Together

The key isn't just having these resources; it's using them effectively. Here's your game plan:
1. Assessment
    a. Identify your academic weak spots.

  b. Know your learning style.

  c. Understand your schedule challenges.

  d. Be honest about where you need help.

2. Resource selection

  a. Choose tools that fit your needs.

  b. Pick apps you'll actually use.

  c. Set up systems that work with your schedule.

  d. Keep it simple and effective.

3. Implementation

  a. Start using resources before you need them.

  b. Build them into your daily routine.

  c. Track what works and what doesn't.

  d. Adjust as needed.

Remember: Using academic resources isn't a sign of weakness; it's a sign of intelligence. The smartest players aren't the ones who know everything; they're the ones who know how to get the help they need to succeed.

Professional teams have entire departments dedicated to player development. College programs have academic support staff. High schools have counselors and teachers willing to help. Use them. These people aren't just doing their jobs; they're investing in your success.

The bottom line? Don't try to be a hero and do everything alone. Use every resource available. Because at the end of the day, your transcript won't show which tools you used to get those grades; it'll just show the grades, and those grades will open or close doors for your future.

Be smart. Be strategic. Use your resources. That's what champions do.

The Long Game

Let's talk about something that might be uncomfortable to think about right now: Football will end. Whether after high school, college, or a 15-year NFL career, at some point, you'll play your last snap. And when that day comes, what you've done in the classroom will matter more than anything you ever did on the field.

Life Beyond the Lines

Here's a reality check: The average NFL career lasts 3.3 years. Even if you make it—and that's a big if—you're looking at retiring in your mid-'20s. Then what? You've got another 40—50 years of life ahead of you. That's why your education isn't just about staying eligible; it's about preparing for your entire life.

Think about some of the NFL greats and what they did after football:

- Alan Page went from the Vikings' defensive line to becoming a State Supreme Court Justice.

- Myron Rolle played safety for the Titans, then became a neurosurgeon.

- Jack Kemp went from quarterback to Secretary of Housing and Urban Development.

These men understood something crucial: Football opens doors, but education keeps them open.

Building Your Professional Playbook

The skills you're developing as a student-athlete are what employers want exactly:

- time management from balancing sports and studies

- leadership from team experiences
- performance under pressure from game situations
- goal-setting and achievement from athletic training
- teamwork from playing a team sport

But here's the catch: These skills only matter if you have the academic credentials to get through the door. Your athletic experience makes you unique, but your education makes you qualified.

The Education Advantage

Let's talk numbers:

- College graduates earn about $1 million more over their lifetime than high school graduates (Egan, 2023).
- The unemployment rate for college graduates is consistently half that of high school graduates (*How Does a College Degree Improve*, 2022).
- Almost 65% of all jobs require some form of post-secondary education (Degnan, 2023).

And here's something else to consider: Many of the most successful people in sports aren't players; they're owners, general managers, agents, and executives. Do you know what they all have in common? Strong educational backgrounds.

Your Post-Playing Options

With a solid education, your options after football are limitless:

- sports management
- coaching

- broadcasting
- business leadership
- entrepreneurship
- law
- medicine
- teaching
- technology
- other options

Each of these paths requires different academic preparation, but they all require one thing: taking your education seriously now.

The Compound Effect

Think of your education like compound interest in a bank account. Every class you take seriously, every concept you master, and every skill you develop are all investments in your future. They might not seem significant now, but they add up over time.

And just like in football, small advantages compound into big ones:

1. Better grades lead to better colleges.
2. Better colleges lead to better opportunities.
3. Better opportunities lead to more options.
4. More options lead to greater success.

The Ultimate Victory

The real win isn't just making it to the next level in football; it's setting yourself up for success in life because while football can make you a living, education can build you a life.

Remember this: The same discipline, focus, and dedication you bring to football? Bring that to your education because while your highlights might live on YouTube, your impact on the world will come from what you do with your entire life, not just your playing career.

Therefore, your education isn't just a backup plan; it's your game plan for life. Treat it with the same respect you give to your athletic training. Because long after the crowds stop cheering and the lights go dark, your education will still be working for you.

That's the long game. And that's the game you can't afford to lose.

The Final Warning

The lesson for all aspiring athletes: Handle your classroom business. It may not seem important now, but your grades will open doors that your skill alone cannot. Higher grades make you eligible for recruitment by more schools. For college players, if you don't make it through four years, getting drafted becomes much harder. Trust me, I had to learn this the hard way, and it wasn't pretty.

Key Takeaways

Before we move on to training strategies, let's lock in what matters most from this chapter:

1. Grades aren't just numbers; they're opportunities. Every assignment, every test, and every class is a chance to open doors for your future. Don't waste these chances.

2. Your academic record tells a story about who you are. Make sure it's telling the right one. Coaches, recruiters, and future employers will all read this story.

3. No matter how talented you are, academics matter. I learned this lesson the hard way, so you don't have to. There are no exceptions to this rule.

Your Action Items

Right now—not tomorrow, not next week—right now, you need to:

1. Conduct a grade check:

    a. Calculate your current GPA.

    b. Identify any classes where you're struggling.

    c. List all upcoming assignments and tests.

2. Build your academic team:

    a. Meet with your teachers–professors.

    b. Connect with tutors if needed.

    c. Find your study group.

3. Create your academic game plan:

    a. Set specific grade goals for each class.

    b. Schedule your study blocks.

    c. Plan your assignment completion dates.

The Bridge to Excellence

As we move into our next chapter about training strategies, remember this: The discipline you build in the classroom impacts your performance on the field directly. The focus you develop while studying helps you learn plays faster. The time management skills you master while handling schoolwork make you more efficient in your training.

Think about it: If you can't handle your business in the classroom, how can coaches trust you to handle your business on the field? If you can't stay focused during a one-hour class, how will you maintain focus during a four-hour practice?

Everything connects. Everything matters. Your success in one area feeds your success in others.

Next up, we're going to dive deep into training strategies that will set you apart from the competition. But as you read about cutting-edge workout techniques and advanced training methods, remember that none of it matters if you're academically ineligible.

Handle your classroom business first. Then, we can talk about dominating on the field.

Let's get to work.

Chapter 3:
Training Like a Champion

For those who know me, they know I'm all about the offseason. One particular offseason—just four weeks—changed my whole life. The offseason is where the regular season is won. It's not just about you; it's about doing the work to be the best you can be for yourself and your team. If you don't improve over the summer while your teammates do, you'll let them down when it counts because you'll be unprepared. The *in-season* is where you maintain your off-season progress, showcase your skills, and compete each week. Thus, the offseason should be hard and tough so that when game time comes, it's easy and fun.

The Truth About Greatness

Here's what most players don't understand: Champions aren't crowned under Friday night lights. They're made in empty weight rooms at 6

a.m. They're forged on deserted fields under the summer sun. They're built in those moments when nobody's watching, nobody's cheering, and the only motivation is the burning desire to be great.

Think about this: Every highlight reel play you've ever seen was made possible by thousands of repetitions nobody witnessed. Every touchdown celebration was earned through countless hours of silent work. Every game-winning moment was created months before, when other players were sleeping or taking it easy.

The offseason isn't just a time between games; it's your opportunity to transform. It's your chance to rebuild yourself from the ground up, to fix weaknesses, and to turn good qualities into great ones and great ones into unstoppable weapons. This is where you build the foundation that will either support your dreams or crumble under pressure.

Let me show you how to make every minute of your offseason count. Because when you do this right, when you truly commit to the process I'm about to share with you, the season becomes the easy part. The games become your chance to show the world what you've been building in silence.

Are you ready to work?

The Foundation Period

The offseason is crucial for athletes. It's the time to address weaknesses and sharpen strengths to elevate your game. During this period, you're probably not fully developed, so you'll spend the first few months in the gym either putting on weight or slimming down while building strength and power. This phase isn't just essential for growth; it's mandatory to prevent injuries and prepare for the next stages of your training.

Building Your Base

Think of your offseason like constructing a skyscraper. You can't start with the penthouse; you need a foundation that can support everything you're going to build. This is where most athletes go wrong. They want to jump straight into the flashy stuff: the one-handed catches, the explosive plays, and the highlight reel moments. But without a proper base, you're building a house of cards that will collapse when the pressure hits.

Understanding the Training Phases

Your off-season training isn't just random workouts thrown together. It's a scientific progression designed to peak at the right time. Here's how it breaks down:

- Phase 1—foundation (weeks 1–4): This is where we build your engine. Everything starts with basic strength and conditioning. You might not see dramatic changes during this phase, but trust the process. We're laying the groundwork that will support everything else.

- Phase 2—development (weeks 5–8): Here, we start adding power to that strength. This is where your explosiveness begins to develop. Your body is adapting, getting stronger, and preparing for the intense work ahead.

- Phase 3—specialization (weeks 9–12): This is when we turn that raw power into football-specific abilities. Every exercise and drill directly translates to your position and goals.

Setting Realistic Goals

Here's the thing about goals: They need to be both ambitious and achievable. I'm not here to tell you to dream small, but I am here to help you build a realistic pathway to those dreams.

Let's start with your daily grind: your process goals. These are the bricks that build your house. These are the things you can control every single day, no matter what. When you say, "I will complete every scheduled workout" or, "I will maintain perfect form on every rep," you're making promises to yourself that you can keep regardless of what anyone else does. These aren't about being perfect; they're about being consistent.

I remember when I was coming up, I set a process goal to catch 100 balls every day after practice. Rain or shine. Tired or fresh. Good practice or bad practice. Some days, those catches were easy. Some days, my hands were burning, and every catch hurt. But that consistency? That daily commitment? That's what separated me from players who only worked when they felt like it.

Next, come your performance goals. These are your measuring sticks. When you say you want to add 30 lbs to your squat max or cut your 40-yd dash time by 0.2 seconds, you're giving yourself clear targets to hit. These goals need to stretch you but not break you. If your squat max is 200 lbs, trying to add 100 lbs in a month isn't realistic. But 30 lbs over 3 months of solid training? That's something you can achieve with consistent work.

Think of performance goals as stepping stones across a river. Each one needs to be within reach of the last one but still push you to stretch. Too close together, and you're not challenging yourself. Too far apart, and you'll fall in the water.

Then, there are your outcome goals: your big dreams. *Earn a starting position. Lead the team in receptions. Get a Division I scholarship.* These are your mountaintops, your ultimate destinations. But here's what most players get wrong about outcome goals: They focus on them too much and their process goals too little.

Mental Preparation

This might be the most overlooked aspect of off-season training, but it's crucial. The offseason is as much a mental challenge as a physical one. Thus, you need to prepare your mind for the grind ahead.

First, understand this isn't going to be easy. There will be days when your body screams to stop, when the weights feel heavier than ever, or when the summer heat becomes unbearable. These moments aren't obstacles; they're opportunities. They're chances to separate yourself from everyone else who's taking it easy.

In this context, develop your mental toughness through:

- visualization of your goals
- daily affirmations of your commitment
- breaking large goals into smaller, manageable chunks
- celebrating small victories while staying hungry for more

Remember: Mental preparation isn't about eliminating doubt or fear. It's about pushing through despite it. Every champion has doubts. Every great player faces fear. The difference is they don't let these feelings stop them.

The Foundation Mindset

As you begin this journey, adopt these key principles:

- Patience with the process
- Trust in the plan
- Consistency over intensity
- Focus on form before weight
- Recovery is as important as work

Think of every rep, every set, and every workout as a brick in your foundation. You're not just building a better athlete; you're building a better you. The habits you form now, the discipline you develop, and the work ethic you establish will serve you not just in football but in life.

Nutrition and Hydration

Habits formed during the offseason will benefit you on your journey. This includes eating properly and hydrating. Many people underestimate the difference this makes, but it's significant. Eating healthy foods maximizes your gains and progress. I weighed 190 lbs in my first 2 seasons despite working out daily because I was eating cafeteria junk food. I should have focused on healthier choices like vegetables and grilled chicken breast. If you want to be a pro athlete, you have to act like one. Be serious about it!

Hydration is key to flushing out toxins and keeping your body loose, which helps prevent injuries. A simple method is to carry a 4-L milk jug filled with water and sip from it all day. One jug a day is the goal. Additionally, stretching is vital. If you're not stretching daily, you're not maximizing your potential. I promise: Stretch every day for 30 minutes for a week, and you'll notice a difference when you run.

The Science of Fueling a Champion

Let me break this down in a way that will change how you think about food forever. Your body isn't just a machine; it's a high-performance vehicle. You wouldn't put regular gas in a Ferrari, so why are you putting junk food in your body?

Meal Timing: The When Matters as Much as the What

Your body needs fuel at specific times to maximize performance:

1. Pre-workout (2–3 hours prior)

    a. Complex carbs for sustained energy

    b. Moderate protein

    c. Low fat to prevent sluggishness. Example: oatmeal with banana and protein shake

2. Post-workout (within 30 minutes)

    a. Fast-acting carbs to replenish glycogen

    b. High-quality protein for muscle recovery

    c. The *golden window* for nutrition. Example: protein shake with fruit and honey

3. Throughout the day

    a. Breakfast sets your metabolic tone.

    b. Small, frequent meals maintain energy.

    c. Never go more than four hours without eating.

Portion Control for Performance

Here's a simple way to portion your meals:
- protein: palm-sized portion—30–40g
- carbs: cupped hand—depending on goals
- vegetables: two fists full
- healthy fats: thumb-sized portion

For gaining mass:
- Increase portions gradually.
- Add calories through quality foods.
- Track progress weekly.

For leaning out:
- Maintain protein intake.
- Reduce carbs strategically.
- Never crash diet.

Supplementation: The Truth

Let's clear up the confusion about supplements. They're exactly what the name suggests: supplements to a good diet, not replacements. Here's what you actually need:
- essential supplements
    - protein powder—for convenience
    - multivitamin—insurance policy

- - creatine monohydrate—proven performance
- optional based on needs
  - pre-workout—be careful with caffeine
  - BCAAs—during intense training
  - fish oil—joint health

Everything else? Save your money for quality food.

Common Nutrition Mistakes and How to Avoid Them

- The timing trap
  - Wrong: Skipping breakfast; huge late-night meals.
  - Right: Eating within an hour of waking; tapering portions toward evening.
- The quality error
  - Wrong: Empty calories from processed foods.
  - Right: Nutrient-dense whole foods.
- The hydration mistake
  - Wrong: Waiting until you're thirsty.
  - Right: Consistent water intake throughout the day.
- The recovery blunder
  - Wrong: Skipping post-workout nutrition.
  - Right: Immediate post-workout refueling.

Creating Your Nutrition Game Plan

Weekly prep

- Sunday meal prep for the week.
- Pack snacks for school–training.
- Prepare your water jug each night.
- Keep emergency protein bars handy.

Remember this: Every meal is either helping you or hurting you. There's no neutral ground when you're pursuing excellence. The same discipline that makes you run that extra sprint or push that extra rep needs to apply to your nutrition.

The best part about proper nutrition? It's one of the few areas where you can have a 100% success rate. You can't control everything that happens on the field, but you can control everything that goes into your body.

Daily Structure for Success

Create a daily schedule to keep yourself committed. For example:

- 6:00 a.m.: Stretch for 30 minutes.
- 6:30 a.m.: Go for a jog.
- 7:30 a.m.: Shower and cook breakfast (e.g., four eggs, avocado with toast, bacon, oatmeal, and a protein shake).
- 9:00 a.m.: Gym session for two hours.
- 11:30 a.m.: Shower and cook lunch (e.g., chicken, broccoli, and fruit).

Beyond the Basic Schedule

Let's talk about what makes a schedule work in the real world because life isn't perfect, and plans don't always go smoothly. The key isn't just having a schedule; it's knowing how to stick to it when life throws you curveballs.

Adapting to Your Situation

Different situations require different approaches. Here's how to make this work for you:

- school days

    o Move morning workouts earlier if needed.

    o Use lunch periods for extra meals.

    o Stack homework and recovery time.

    o Plan around team lifts and practices.

- working a job

    o Communicate your training needs early with employers.

    o Use breaks strategically for meals.

    o Combine cardio with commuting when possible.

    o Maximize weekend training.

- living at home

    o Get family buy-in for your schedule.

    o Prep meals in bulk to help with family cooking.

    o Create a dedicated training space.

- Set boundaries around training time.

Weekend Warriors

Weekends aren't for slacking; they're for getting ahead. Here's your weekend game plan:

- Saturday
    - longer training sessions
    - meal prep for the week
    - extra skill work
    - recovery protocols
- Sunday
    - light active recovery
    - schedule planning for the week
    - film study
    - mental preparation

Managing Disruptions

Life will try to derail your training. Here's how to stay on track when you face unexpected events:

1. Have backup workouts ready:
    a. Twenty-minute hotel room circuits
    b. Body weight alternatives
    c. Quick mobility routines

2. Nutrition emergency kit:

    a. Protein bars

    b. Mixed nuts

    c. Protein shakes

    d. Fruit

3. Time crunch solutions:

    a. Combine cardio with commuting

    b. Super-set workouts to save time

    c. Meal prep in bulk

    d. Use *dead time* for stretching–mobility

Creating Your Power Hours

Identify your nonnegotiable training blocks:
- morning ritual (30–45 minutes)
- primary training (60–120 minutes)
- Recovery–mobility (30 minutes)
- Meal prep (45 minutes)

These blocks move around your schedule, but they never disappear.

The Success System

Build habits that support your schedule:

1. Night-before preparation

a. Lay out training clothes.

   b. Pack meals and snacks.

   c. Review the next day's schedule.

   d. Set multiple alarms.

2. Morning jump start

   a. Immediate hydration

   b. Quick mobility work

   c. Mental focus moment

   d. Nutrition first

3. Daily check-ins

   a. Monitor energy levels.

   b. Track completion of tasks.

   c. Adjust as needed.

   d. Plan for tomorrow.

Remember: A schedule isn't about being perfect; it's about being consistent. The goal isn't to never miss; it's to never miss twice. When disruptions come—and they will—don't abandon the plan; adjust it. Success isn't built on perfect days; it's built on responding perfectly to imperfect ones.

Your schedule is your blueprint for success. Protect it. Honor it. But most importantly, make it work for you. Because at the end of the day, the best schedule is the one you'll actually follow.

The Off-Season Blueprint

You should be working out at least once a day, with one or two rest days for recovery. A minimum of five times a week is essential. Remember, someone out there is working hard—don't let them outwork you. For the first two months, focus on strength and size. In the last month, shift to speed and power—lifting heavy weights quickly and explosively—along with plyometric jumps and hops. After two to three months of consistent weight training, you should see progress and new personal records.

The Evolution of a Champion

The offseason isn't just a time period; it's a transformation process. Think of it like building a house. You don't start with the roof; you start with the foundation. Each month builds upon the previous one, creating something stronger, more powerful, and more resilient than before.

Let me break down how this evolution happens, month by month, and show you exactly what it takes to transform yourself from a good athlete into a great one.

Month 1: The Foundation

Your first month is all about building your base. This is where most athletes go wrong: They want to jump straight into the flashy stuff, the explosive movements, and the highlight-reel training. But that's like trying to sprint before you can walk.

During this phase, you're focusing on fundamental movement patterns. Heavy compound lifts form the core of your training. We're talking squats, dead lifts, bench presses, and rows. But here's the key: It's not about how much weight you're moving. It's about how well you're moving it.

Every rep should be perfect. Every set should be focused. You're not just building strength; you're building movement patterns that will serve as the foundation for everything that follows.

Month 2: The Builder

Now that your foundation is solid, we start adding layers. This is where the real transformation begins. The weights get heavier, the workouts get more intense, and your body starts to adapt to the demands you're placing on it.

Think of this month as forging steel. The heat gets turned up, and you're reshaped into something stronger. Your workouts become more complex. We start combining movements, adding explosive elements after your strength work, and introducing position-specific drills.

This is also where mental toughness becomes crucial. The workouts are harder, longer, and more demanding. You'll have days where everything in your body is screaming to stop. These are the moments that separate good athletes from great ones.

Month 3: The Power Phase

This is where everything comes together. All that foundational strength, all those perfect movement patterns, and all the mental toughness you've built get channeled into explosive power.

Your training now becomes more dynamic. Olympic lift variations teach you to generate force quickly. Plyometrics help you translate that force into athletic movements. Position-specific work ensures that all this new power directly improves your game performance.

Position-Specific Excellence

Football isn't a one-size-fits-all sport. A quarterback needs different qualities than a lineman. A receiver's training should look different from a linebacker's. But the principles remain the same; it's how we apply them that changes.

- For receivers and DBs, we emphasize single-leg power and change of direction. Your training should mirror the demands of your position—quick accelerations, sudden stops, explosive jumps.

- Linemen need raw power combined with quick bursts of energy. Your training focuses on explosive power from the ground up, building the strength to dominate the line of scrimmage.

- Quarterbacks require a unique blend of rotational power and precision. Your training emphasizes core stability, shoulder health, and the ability to generate force while maintaining accuracy.

Tracking Your Transformation

Progress isn't just about feeling better; it's about knowing better. Every week, you should be tracking key metrics. Your main lifts should be recorded. Your body composition should be monitored. Your performance markers should be measured.

But here's what most people miss: It's not just about the numbers. It's about how those numbers are trending over time. Are you getting stronger while maintaining speed? Is your power increasing without sacrificing mobility? These are the questions that matter.

Remember this: The offseason is your time to build yourself into something special. Every workout is a brick in the foundation of your success. Every rep is an investment in your future. You're not just training; you're transforming.

The question isn't whether you can do it. The question is: Are you willing to do what it takes, day after day, week after week, to become the athlete you know you can be?

Speed Development

January is when track work comes into play. If your school has a track club or you have access to a speed trainer, this is the time to leverage it with your new strength. Track and field training is the key to elite speed. Sprint at least two to three times a week while continuing to lift. If possible, compete in local track meets to boost intensity and maximize your speed.

The Science of Speed

Here's something most football players don't understand: Speed isn't just about running fast. It's a skill that can be developed, refined, and mastered. Just like you practice your routes or your tackles, you need to practice the art of speed.

Think about speed like building a sports car. Raw power (strength) is your engine, but without proper mechanics (technique), aerodynamics (form), and a skilled driver (nervous system), that power goes to waste. Let's break down how to build your speed the right way.

Sprint Mechanics: The Foundation of Speed

Everything starts with proper mechanics. You could have all the power in the world, but with poor form, you'll leak speed like a car with a bad transmission. Here's what elite speed looks like:

1. The drive phase: Your first 10–15 yd are all about explosive power. Your body should be at a 45° angle, driving hard into the ground. Every step is like trying to push the earth away from you. Your arms should be pumping explosively, driving your knees up with each stride.

2. The transition phase: As you move from acceleration to top speed, your body gradually rises to an upright position. This is where most athletes lose speed—they rise too quickly or too

slowly. The key is a smooth, gradual transition while maintaining power output.

3. Top speed phase: Now, you're upright but not rigid. Think *tall and relaxed*. Your arms should swing naturally from hip to face. Your feet should be striking directly under your center of mass, not reaching out in front of you.

Acceleration: The Game-Changer

In football, it's rarely about top speed; it's about how quickly you can reach your speed. Here's how we develop explosive acceleration:

1. Start position: Whether you're in a three-point stance or standing, your first movement should explode forward, not up. Think about driving out, not standing up.

2. First three steps: These are your moneymakers. Each step should be powerful and aggressive, with your foot striking back against the ground, not reaching forward. Your arm drive should be violent but controlled.

3. Force production: Every step should feel like you're trying to push the ground behind you. The more force you put into the ground, the more speed you'll get back.

Building Speed Endurance

Raw speed is great, but football demands repeated sprints with minimal recovery. Here's how we build that capacity:

- Progressive volume: Start with shorter sprints—10–20 yd—with full recovery. Gradually increase distance and decrease rest periods as your conditioning improves.

- Tempo work: Not every sprint needs to be at 100%. Running at 70–80% helps build proper mechanics and endurance without overly taxing your nervous system.

- Recovery capacity: Work on your ability to recover between sprints. Practice controlling your breathing and staying relaxed even when fatigued.

Position-Specific Speed Training

Your position determines how you need to express your speed on the field:

- Receivers–DBs: Focus on acceleration out of breaks, maintaining speed through direction changes, and the ability to accelerate while tracking the ball.

- Linemen: Emphasize 10-yd explosion, lateral quickness, and the ability to maintain speed while engaged with opponents.

- Running backs: Work on acceleration through traffic, speed maintenance through cuts, and burst out-of-direction changes.

Remember: True speed development takes time and patience. You won't get faster overnight, but with consistent, proper training, you will get faster. Every sprint rep is an opportunity to ingrain proper mechanics and build that mind-muscle connection that turns raw power into explosive speed.

The key is quality over quantity. Five perfect sprints are better than fifteen sloppy ones. Each rep should be focused, intentional, and explosive. Moreover, rest fully between reps; speed training isn't conditioning. You need to be fresh enough to execute with perfect form every time.

Preseason Preparation

The last 2–3 months before the season should be spent on field training and maintaining gym sessions. This is where you test your *new Ferrari* on the track. You'll need to focus on body control to get comfortable starting, stopping, and bursting in and out of cuts. The field phase emphasizes fundamentals for 3 months. Set a goal of 10,000 routes and 10,000 catches—it sounds extreme, but it adds up. Run routes until your toenails bleed if you have to. The more comfortable you are running and breaking at different angles, the better your route running becomes. Work on getting out of breaks in 3 steps or fewer.

Mastering Your Craft

Now is when everything you've built in the weight room gets translated to football-specific excellence. Think of it like this: you've built the engine, and now it's time to learn how to drive. This phase is about turning raw athletic ability into football mastery.

Technical Excellence

Your technique needs to become automatic. Under pressure, in the fourth quarter, when you're exhausted, your form needs to hold up. This only happens through relentless repetition.

1. Start with the basics: Every day starts with fundamental drills. If you're a receiver, that means catching 100 balls before you even begin route work. If you're a DB, it's backpedal drills until they're perfect. Linemen, it's foot fire and hand placement drills.

2. Build complexity gradually: Once basics are solid, add layers of difficulty. Work against air, then cones, then bags, then live opponents. Each step builds on the last, creating muscle memory that holds up under game conditions.

3. Perfect practice makes perfect: Every rep needs to be game speed. Every movement needs to be precise. You're not just going through the motions; you're programming excellence into your nervous system.

Position Mastery

This is where you become a student of your position. Study films of the greats. Break down their movements. Understand why they succeeded.

- for receivers
    - Master the subtle head fake.
    - Perfect the first three steps off the line.
    - Develop multiple release techniques.
    - Learn to maintain speed through breaks.
- for defensive backs
    - Perfect your backpedal.
    - Master hip transitions.
    - Develop recognition skills.
    - Learn to play through the hands.
- for linemen
    - Master your stance.
    - Perfect your first step.
    - Develop hand-fighting techniques.
    - Learn to read blocking schemes.

Game Simulation

Now, we put it all together in gamelike conditions. This is where you test everything you've built under pressure.

- Create game scenarios: Set up situations you'll face in games. Fourth and long. Red zone. Two-minute drill. Practice them until they feel routine.

- Add pressure: Work against defenders. Add noise. Create distractions. Make practice harder than games.

- Build endurance: Run your routes or drills when you're tired. The perfect form has to hold up in the fourth quarter.

The Mental Game

Preseason isn't just physical preparation; it's mental warfare training.

- Visualization: Before every practice session, visualize perfect execution. See yourself succeeding. Feel the movements in your mind before you make them with your body.

- Building confidence: Each successful rep builds confidence. Each mastered technique adds to your arsenal. By game time, you should know—not think, but know—that you can execute under pressure.

- Focus training: Practice maintaining focus through distractions. Learn to narrow your concentration to what matters at the moment.

Integration Work

This final phase brings everything together:
- strength from the weight room

- speed from track work

- technique from skill training

- mental toughness from preparation

The key is seamless integration. Every movement should feel natural. Every technique should be automatic. You're not thinking anymore; you're reacting with trained excellence.

The preseason is your dress rehearsal for greatness. Every detail matters. Every rep counts. You're not just preparing for the season; you're preparing for those crucial moments when games are won and lost.

In-Season Excellence

Now, it's showtime. Everything you've done in the offseason prepares you for this. Establish a routine that works for you. For example, if you have practice Monday through Thursday with a game on Friday, plan your training and weight sessions around this schedule. Train legs the day after the game, focusing on light squats to get them right while allowing recovery time before practice. Do speed training–fieldwork on the first practice day of the week so your legs have time to rest and recover before game day.

The in-season isn't a time to be lazy; it's even more intense than the offseason. How good do you want to be? During practice, treat every rep as if it's game day. Aim to improve at least one thing each practice. Be critical when watching practice and game films—it's your answer key before the test. In this setting, break down your film to find weak spots to work on. Be your biggest critic because you won't always have someone else to do it. And don't be embarrassed to work on your weaknesses; reps will turn them into strengths.

The Championship Routine

Let's dive deeper into what in-season excellence really looks like. This isn't just about maintaining what you built in the offseason; it's about continuing to improve when the pressure is highest.

The Weekly Blueprint

Think of each week as its own mini-season. Here's how to master the rhythm of game weeks:

1. Sunday: recovery and analysis

    a. Light movement to flush out soreness

    b. Initial film review from Friday's game

    c. Mental preparation for the week ahead

    d. Mobility work and injury prevention

2. Monday: installation and building

    a. New game plan installation

    b. Technical work at 80% speed

c. Core and upper body maintenance

   d. Extra film study on new opponents

3. Tuesday: power and precision

   a. Full-speed position work

   b. Explosive movement training

   c. Situational mastery

   d. Opposition study

4. Wednesday: peak performance prep

   a. Fine-tuning game plan execution

   b. Speed maintenance work

   c. Mental visualization

   d. Position group film study

5. Thursday: sharp and ready

   a. Quick, crisp walk-through

   b. Mental preparation

   c. Light activation work

   d. Final game plan review

6. Friday: game day

   a. Focused morning routine

   b. Clear mental approach

   c. Precise warm-up

d. Game time excellence

Maintaining Your Gains

The biggest mistake athletes make in-season is completely abandoning their strength work. You don't need to lift as heavy or as often, but you need to maintain what you've built. Here's how:

- strength maintenance
    - Two quality sessions per week.
    - Focus on key movement patterns.
    - Maintain intensity and reduce volume.
    - Listen to your body's recovery needs.
- speed work
    - short, explosive bursts
    - quality over quantity
    - perfect technique emphasis
    - recovery-conscious approach

Game Preparation Mastery

Your preparation determines your performance. Develop a game-day routine that becomes second nature:

- pregame study
    - Know your opponent's tendencies.
    - Understand your assignments cold.

- Visualize your success.
            - Review key situations.
    - physical preparation
        - consistent sleep schedule
        - proper hydration protocol
        - specific warm-up routine
        - energy management
    - mental readiness
        - quiet confidence building
        - focus techniques
        - pressure management
        - performance triggers

The Extra Edge

What separates good players from great ones isn't just what they do during team activities; it's what they do beyond the required work:

- extra film study
    - Break down your own performance.
    - Study elite players at your position.
    - Learn opponent tendencies.
    - Understand whole-game concepts.

- skill enhancement
    - extra catches after practice
    - footwork refinement
    - hand-eye coordination work
    - position-specific drills
- recovery excellence
    - active recovery protocols
    - proper nutrition timing
    - sleep optimization
    - stress management

In-season excellence isn't about doing more; it's about doing the right things at the right time. Every day should have a purpose. Every practice should make you better. Every game should be an opportunity to showcase your preparation.

You're not just playing games now; you're building your legacy. Each week is a chance to prove that your off-season work wasn't just for show. This is where champions separate themselves from the rest.

The season is a grind, but it's also an opportunity. An opportunity to prove yourself, to improve yourself, and to push yourself beyond what you thought possible. Embrace the process. Trust your preparation. Execute your plan.

Game time isn't just showtime; it's *prove it* time. And you've got to prove it every single week.

Recovery Mastery

Recovery during the season is crucial. It's often the difference between staying healthy and getting injured. While injuries can be unpredictable, recovery plays a significant role. To achieve this, hydration and refueling your body with calories are key. Aim for 1 gal of water a day and always eat after physical activity to maintain weight and energy.

The Science of Recovery

Let me tell you something that took me years to learn: Recovery isn't just rest; it's an active process that's just as important as training itself. Think of it like this: Training breaks you down; recovery builds you up. And if you're not building up faster than you're breaking down, you're moving backward, not forward.

Your body is like a high-performance car. You can't run it at full throttle all the time and expect it to last. You need to maintain it, tune it, and sometimes, let it cool down. That's what smart recovery is all about.

Sleep: Your Secret Weapon

The best recovery tool isn't in the training room; it's your bed. I used to think sleep was for the weak. Man, was I wrong. Everything happens in your sleep: muscle repair, hormone production, and mental recovery. It's when your body does its most important work.

Create a sleep sanctuary. Your room should be dark, cool, and quiet. Think of it as your recovery cave. The hours before midnight are golden; they're worth double in terms of recovery. Get to bed early, and make it a nonnegotiable part of your routine.

Active Recovery: The Missing Link

Here's what separates the pros from the amateurs: pros understand that recovery isn't about doing nothing. It's about doing the right things at the right time. When you're sore after a game, the worst thing you can do is sit around all day. Your body needs movement—smart, purposeful movement.

Get in the pool. Take a light jog. Do some yoga. Movement promotes blood flow, and blood flow promotes healing. Think of it like cleaning out your system – you're flushing out the damage and bringing in the repair crew.

Injury Prevention: The Smart Approach

The best ability is availability. I learned this the hard way. You can be the most talented player in the world, but if you're always injured, that talent means nothing. Note that prevention isn't about avoiding activity; it's about preparing your body for what's coming.

Listen to your body's whispers before they become shouts. That little twinge in your hamstring? Address it now. That slight stiffness in your shoulder? Don't ignore it. Your body is constantly talking to you, so learn to listen.

To accomplish this, develop a relationship with your body. Understand its signals. Know when to push and when to back off. This isn't being soft; it's being smart. The toughest players I know are also the most in tune with their bodies.

Recovery isn't what you do when you're hurt; it's what you do to stay healthy. It's not a sign of weakness; it's a sign of wisdom. The players who last, stay healthy, and perform when it matters most are usually not the ones who train the hardest. They're the ones who recover the smartest.

Make recovery your competitive advantage. Because when everyone else is breaking down at the end of the season, you'll be hitting your stride.

The Champion's Mindset

The takeaway: If you want to be the best, you have to outwork the rest. It's going to be hard, painful, and exhausting. But how bad do you want it? More than a video game? More than hanging out with friends? More than sleep? Stay focused—it's what it takes.

Beyond the Physical

Let's be real for a moment. Everything we've talked about in this chapter—the training, the nutrition, the recovery—comes down to one thing: your mind. The weights don't care about your dreams. The field doesn't know about your goals. The only thing that matters is what you're willing to do when everything in your body is screaming to stop.

Think about every great player you've ever watched. What separates them isn't just talent; it's their mindset. They approach every workout, every practice, and every rep like it's their last. They understand that excellence isn't an act but a habit. They don't just work hard when they feel like it; they work hard because that's who they are.

This is the mindset you need to develop. Every time you choose the gym over the couch, every time you pick water over soda, and every time you do one more rep when you could have stopped, you're not just building your body but your character.

As we move into our next chapter about recruiting, remember this: Recruiters aren't just looking at your performance; they're looking at your process. They want to know if you have the mindset of a champion because talent might get you noticed, but it's your mindset that will get you recruited.

The question isn't whether you can do it. The question is: Are you willing to do what others won't to achieve what others can't?

Let's find out.

Chapter 4:
Navigating Recruitment

Recruiting is one of those topics that not many truly understand. In Canada, specifically, there's a common belief among players that offers will just fall from the sky without any work. Don't get me wrong, if you're a 6'5", 220-lbs receiver running a 4.4, then yes, offers will likely come your way. But for everyone else, you're going to have to work for those offers like everybody else.

The Truth About Your Journey

Let me tell you something that might be hard to hear: Your highlight reel isn't enough. Your stats aren't enough. Even your talent might not be enough. In today's recruiting landscape, you need to be your own advocate, your own agent, and your own marketing team. Nobody is going to do this work for you.

Think about these numbers for a second: There are roughly 1.1 million high school football players in America, let alone around the world, and a very small percentage will play college football at any level. And Division I ? Those odds are even smaller. This isn't meant to discourage you; it's meant to wake you up to the reality of what you're facing.

Let that sink in. Look around your team. Look at every player you compete against on Friday nights. Most of them dream of playing college ball. But wishing and dreaming won't get you there. You need a plan. You need to work. You need to hustle.

Here's what most players are doing:
- waiting for coaches to find them
- hoping their film speaks for itself
- thinking their stats will get them noticed
- believing talent alone is enough

Here's what successful recruits are doing:
- taking control of their process
- building relationships with coaches
- marketing themselves consistently
- working the system smart, not just hard

But here's the good news: While most players are sitting around waiting to be discovered, you're about to learn exactly how to take control of your recruiting journey. This chapter isn't about sugarcoating the process or telling you what you want to hear. It's about giving you the real blueprint for getting noticed, getting offers, and getting your shot at the next level.

Think about it like this: If you were trying to get a record deal, would you just post your music online and wait? No. You'd promote yourself. You'd network. You'd get your music in front of the right people. You'd create opportunities. Well, recruiting is no different.

The game has changed. The old days of coaches discovering hidden gems in small towns are mostly gone. In today's world, if you want to play college football, you need to understand the recruiting process like a business. Because that's exactly what it is—a business. And you? You're the product, the marketer, and the salesperson all rolled into one.

What does this mean for you?

- You need to be proactive, not reactive.

- You need to create opportunities, not wait for them.

- You need to stand out, not blend in.

- You need to sell yourself, not just play well.

- You need to be professional, not just talented.

- You need to be persistent, not just patient.

This isn't about being the best player in your area anymore. This is about being the best at getting yourself noticed, being the best at following up, and being the best at making connections. Because here's the truth: Sometimes, the players who get recruited aren't the most talented; they're the ones who understand how the game is really played.

Are you ready to learn how this game is really played? Because what you're about to learn isn't just about getting recruited; it's about taking control of your future. It's about making things happen instead of waiting for them to happen.

The playbook is in your hands. What are you going to do with it?

The Modern Recruitment Landscape

Recruiting today is tough. The transfer portal, politics, and shady recruiting services promising to get your film seen by top programs all play a role in complicating the process. I won't dive deep into those services, but you can probably guess my opinion based on my tone. That said, if you want an offer, you need to put yourself out there and stand out. You're competing with millions of athletes of similar size, weight, and skills. What makes you different? This is what we'll address because it shouldn't be as complicated as people make it out to be.

In 2024, high school scholarships are harder than ever to secure. Schools aren't focusing as much on developing players anymore; they want players who can help the team right away.

The New Reality

Let me break down what today's recruiting landscape really looks like. It's a whole different game than it was even five years ago. The transfer portal has changed everything. Think of it like free agency in the NFL but for college football. Schools can now shop for experienced college players instead of developing high school talent.

What does this mean for you? It means the bar is higher than ever. Schools aren't just comparing you to other high school players anymore; they're comparing you to proven college athletes who are looking to transfer. They're asking themselves: "Should we take a chance on developing this high school player or grab someone who's already proven they can play at college level?"

The Transfer Portal Effect

The transfer portal has created a new dynamic in recruiting. Schools are holding back scholarships, waiting to see which experienced players might become available. This means fewer immediate opportunities for high school players, but it also means you need to be smarter about your approach.

Think of it this way: Schools still need freshman talent—they just need to be more convinced than ever that you're worth the investment. They need to see not just what you are now but what you could become in their program.

Here's what coaches are really thinking about when they look at high school recruits in the transfer portal period:

- Can this player contribute early enough to justify not taking a transfer?

- Does this player have enough potential for growth to make developing them worth the time?

- Is this player worth the risk when experienced players are available?

The Politics of Recruiting

Here's something they don't talk about enough: Recruiting is often political.

- Sometimes, it's about who you know.

- Sometimes, it's about where you're from.

- Sometimes, it's about which other players the school is recruiting.

Understanding this doesn't mean accepting defeat; it means being strategic about where and how you market yourself.

I've seen it firsthand: talented players getting overlooked because they didn't understand the political side of recruiting. But I've also seen players with average talent get opportunities because they understood how to work the system.

The reality is that recruiting isn't just about what you can do on the field. It's about relationships, timing, and seeing the whole picture. You need to know which schools are realistic for you, which coaches to connect with, and how to make yourself stand out.

The Truth About Recruiting Services

Let me be brutally honest here—something that might save you thousands of dollars. Most recruiting services are selling dreams, not reality. They'll promise to get your film in front of every coach in the country. They'll tell you about their *special relationships* with programs. They'll guarantee exposure.

But here's what actually happens: Your film ends up in a digital pile with thousands of others, and coaches still trust their own eyes and relationships more than any third-party service.

I'm not saying all recruiting services are worthless, but you need to understand what they can and can't do. They can't make you faster, stronger, or more talented. They can't make a coach offer you a scholarship. What they can do is help with exposure, but you can do most of that yourself with some hard work and smart strategy.

The Competition Reality

The numbers in football recruiting are eye-opening. You're not just competing against players from your state or even your country anymore. The recruitment landscape has gone global. Canadian players, European players, and Australian players are all in the mix now.

Think about these numbers:

- over a million high school football players in North America

- roughly 130 FBS schools

- about 85 scholarships per school

- only about 25 spots open per year per school on average (Daily Editorials, 2023)

When you do the math, you realize just how competitive this process is. But here's the thing: These numbers shouldn't discourage you. They should motivate you to be more strategic, work harder, and stand out in ways that others aren't willing to.

The path to college football isn't closed; it's just different than it used to be. Understanding this new landscape is your first step toward navigating it successfully. The players who succeed in today's recruitment environment aren't just the most talented; they're the ones who best understand and adapt to this new reality.

Standing Out From the Crowd

First and foremost, your film needs to show dominance. You want to look like a star amongst your peers. If you're a receiver, aim for 100 yd/game with at least 2 deep or catch-and-run touchdowns. High numbers? Yes, but you want to look like a man among boys. Defensive players should aim for a pick and–or big, impactful hits—the type that resonates audibly. If you don't stand out on film, what would give a coach a reason to believe you can perform at the next level?

Appearance matters, too. Do you look like a college player in terms of size and muscle? Or are you underdeveloped and unable to bench 135 lbs? It sounds trivial, but trust me, it matters. Coaches want to know if you can physically dominate the competition. Look at 5-star recruits; they all have impressive physical attributes and appear ready to contribute immediately. This is what sets their stock high.

Now, if you're a smaller player, don't despair. Size alone doesn't make or break your chances. If you're consistent in the gym and physically prepared, there's still an opportunity for you. You'll just need to compensate with other strengths, like heart, speed, or hitting power.

Creating Dominant Film

Let's talk about what *dominance* really means in film. It's not just about making plays; it's about making plays that make coaches rewind the tape and watch again. Every time you step on the field, you need to be thinking about creating moments that can't be ignored.

Position-By-Position Excellence

- Quarterbacks: You need to show more than just a strong arm. Show your ability to read defenses, work through your receiver options, and deliver under pressure. That touchdown pass is great, but coaches want to see you stepping up in the pocket, keeping your eyes downfield, and making the right decision when your first read isn't there.

- Running backs: Breaking long runs is impressive, but show you can create yards in tight spaces. Demonstrate pass protection skills. Show you can catch out of the backfield. Make defenders miss in space, but also demonstrate you can lower your shoulder and get tough yards.

- Receivers–tight ends: Routes need to be crisp. Releases need to be explosive. Show you can win contested catches but also get open. Moreover, block with intensity; coaches love receivers who aren't afraid to get physical in the run game.

- Defensive players: Every play should show your football IQ. Proper pursuit angles, sure tackling, and ability to get past blockers. Big hits are great, but consistent, fundamentally sound play is what coaches really want to see.

The Physical Presence Factor

Looking the part isn't about looks; it's about showing you're ready for the next level. This means:

Building Your Frame

Your body is your billboard. When coaches see you in person, they should see someone who's been putting in serious work in the weight room. This doesn't mean you need to look like a bodybuilder but need to show development appropriate for your position.

Think about position-specific development:

- Linemen need to show core strength and lower body power.

- Skill positions need to show explosiveness and useful muscle.

- Quarterbacks need to show they can absorb hits and maintain durability.

The Development Project

Here's something crucial to understand: Coaches are evaluating not just what you are now but what you could become in their program. They're looking at:

- frame potential—can you carry more good weight?

- current strength levels

- movement patterns

- physical tests—vertical jump, broad jump, etc.

Beyond the Measurables

However, standing out isn't just about physical attributes. It's about the qualities you can't measure that show up on film:

- Leadership: Show you can rally your teammates. Be the guy who picks others up after a bad play. Demonstrate emotional control in tough situations.

- Football IQ: Your film should show you understand the game:

    o Make pre-snap adjustments.

    o Recognize formations.

    o Show you can think on your feet.

- Competitive fire: Play through the whistle. Chase downplays from behind. Show up in big moments. These things tell coaches about your character.

Creating Your Signature

Every great player has something that makes them special—their signature. Maybe it's your ability to high-point the ball. Maybe it's your exceptional open-field tackling. Maybe it's your burst off the line. Find what makes you unique and make sure it shows up consistently on film.

Remember: Standing out isn't about being good at everything; it's about being exceptional at something. Coaches need to be able to envision exactly how you'll contribute to their program.

This is a game of separation. In a pile of highlight tapes that all start to look the same, what makes yours different? What makes a coach stop, rewind, and watch again? What makes them pick up the phone and call your coach?

The answer isn't just in your highlights; it's in the complete package you present. Physical presence, film dominance, and that special something that makes you, you. Put it all together, and now, you're not just another recruit; you're someone they need to take a serious look at.

The Art of Film

Film is another huge part of the recruiting process. The best way to handle it is to compile highlights after each game. By *highlights*, I mean exceptional plays, not the ordinary ones. Make plays that stand out: catches over 2 defenders, breaking tackles and running it 50 yd to the house, or trucking a DB and outrunning the defense. Be honest with yourself, as these highlights should "wow" coaches and show them how you can elevate their team.

Creating Your Story on Film

Think of your highlight reel like a movie trailer: You've got a limited time to grab the viewer's attention and make them want to see more. Just like a Hollywood studio wouldn't put their boring scenes in a trailer, you can't put average plays in your highlights.

Let me tell you about films from a coach's perspective: They're watching hundreds of these. They're busy. They're distracted. You've got about 30 seconds to make them sit up and take notice. After that, you either have their attention, or they're moving on to the next prospect.

Game-By-Game Excellence

Here's what separates good highlight reels from great ones: consistency. Don't just show one great game. Coaches want to see you making plays week after week. After each game, while it's fresh in your mind, break down your best three to five plays immediately. Ask yourself:

- Does this play show something unique about my ability?
- Would this play work at the next level?
- Does this demonstrate football IQ, not just athletic ability?
- Is this better than what's already in my highlight reel?

Selecting Your Best Plays

Be honest with yourself. That 5-yd catch might have felt great at the moment, but does it show college-level ability? Here's what really catches a coach's eye:

- for skill positions
    - plays that show exceptional speed or power
    - demonstrations of top-level catching and ball handling
    - high football IQ moments
    - competitive plays against top competition
- for linemen
    - pancake blocks
    - pass protection against good rushers
    - getting off double teams
    - pursuit plays showing effort and speed
- for defensive players
    - clean, forceful tackles
    - pass breakups showing instincts
    - blitz timing and execution
    - impact plays in crucial moments

The Technical Side

Your plays might be great, but poor video quality can kill your chances. Here's what matters:

- quality
    - clear, stable footage

- multiple angles when possible
- proper speed—no artificially sped-up plays
- clear identification of yourself before each play

- structure
    - Start with your absolute best three plays.
    - Group similar plays together.
    - Show versatility throughout.
    - End strong with impact plays.

Presentation Strategy

Your highlight reel needs to tell your story in a specific way:

1. The opening: The first 30 seconds are crucial. Lead with your most explosive, impressive plays. Make coaches want to keep watching.

2. The flow:

    a. Group similar plays together

    b. Show progression of skills

    c. Show you can do different things

    d. Include game-situation context

3. The details:

    a. Include a clear identifier—jersey number, arrow, etc.

    b. Add simple graphics for context—down and distance, score

    c. Keep transitions clean and professional

d. Avoid excessive effects or music that distracts

Beyond the Highlights

Remember that coaches might ask for a full-game film. Make sure you have it ready. Full games show the following:
- how you perform when tired
- your effort on routine plays
- your behavior after mistakes
- your impact throughout an entire game

The Final Product

Your highlight reel should be:
- three to five minutes maximum for initial submission
- updated regularly with new top plays
- easy to access—Hudl or a similar platform
- downloadable for coaches to share

Remember: Your film is your resume in the football world. Just like you wouldn't turn in a messy school project, don't send out a poorly made highlight reel. Take the time to do it right. Every play you include should serve a purpose: to show coaches exactly how you can help their program win games.

Building Your Recruiting Profile

Your recruiting profile is like your personal brand in the football world. Think of it as your complete story—not just what you do on the field, but who you are as a total student-athlete. Note that coaches aren't just recruiting players; they're recruiting future representatives of their program.

The Academic Foundation

Let's be real about academics for a moment. Your transcript isn't just a bunch of letters and numbers; it's a record of your commitment to excellence off the field. When coaches look at your grades, they're seeing more than just your GPA. They're noticing how you handle responsibility, how you respond to challenges, and whether you're willing to put in work when nobody's watching.

Every "A" on your transcript tells a coach you're someone who pursues excellence. Every challenging course you take shows you're not afraid to push yourself. Think about it: If you're willing to challenge yourself with AP classes and maintain good grades while playing football, that says something about your character.

Test scores matter more than most players realize. A strong ACT or SAT score can be the difference-maker when coaches are deciding between two similar athletes. These scores don't just show intelligence; they show your ability to prepare, perform under pressure, and handle complex tasks. Sound familiar? These are the same qualities coaches want to see on the field.

Beyond Basic Numbers

Academic achievements go beyond just grades and test scores. Are you involved in student leadership? Have you taken part in academic competitions? Do you volunteer in your community? These activities show coaches you're a well-rounded individual who can manage multiple responsibilities—an important skill for college athletics.

Remember, coaches are looking for players who won't be at academic risk. They have limited scholarships and can't afford to give them to players who might become academically ineligible. Hence, your academic profile needs to show them you're a safe bet.

The Physical Profile

Now, let's talk about your physical measurements. These numbers tell a story, too, but it's how you present them that matters. Sure, your height, weight, and speed are important, but coaches want to see progression. Where were you last year? Where are you now? What's your potential for growth?

Your combined numbers need context. A 4.6 forty might not turn heads at a major Division I school, but if you've dropped your time from 4.8 to 4.6 in 6 months, that shows development potential. Coaches love seeing this kind of progression—it tells them you're still growing, still improving, still hungry.

Position-specific metrics matter enormously. If you're a quarterback, your release time and accuracy percentages are essential. Receivers need to show their route-running times and how far they can reach to catch. Linemen need to demonstrate their strength numbers and footwork metrics. These aren't just numbers; they're indicators of your potential impact on their program.

The Development Story

Here's what really makes coaches take notice: your development curve. Track your progress carefully. Keep records of your weight room numbers, speed times, and agility drills. Show them where you started and how far you've come. This isn't just about current abilities; it's about showing coaches your potential for growth in their program.

Create a clear narrative about your physical development. Maybe you were a 165-lbs sophomore who's grown into a 190-lbs senior with room to add more good weight. Maybe you've transformed how your body is built while maintaining your speed. These transformations show coaches you understand how to develop your body and that you're committed to the process.

Putting It All Together

Your complete recruiting profile should tell a strong story about who you are and what you bring to a program. It's not just about being a good athlete or a good student; it's about being someone who can succeed in their program and represent it well.

Think about this: Coaches are essentially investing in your future. They're betting not only that you'll perform on the field but also that you'll graduate, be a positive influence in their program, and make them look good for recruiting you. Your profile needs to give them confidence in making that bet.

The key is authenticity. Don't try to be something you're not. If you're not a 4.4 sprinter, don't claim to be. If your grades aren't perfect, show how you've worked to improve them. Coaches appreciate honesty and evidence of growth more than inflated numbers and empty promises.

Your recruiting profile is something that keeps growing and changing. Keep updating it. Keep improving it. Keep adding to your story. Because in the end, coaches aren't just recruiting what you are; they're recruiting what you could become in their program.

Coach Communication Strategy

Mid-season is when you create your first full highlight reel. Start with your top 5 plays to grab the coach's attention immediately. This will determine if they keep watching or move on to the next athlete. Remember, coaches receive highlights from hundreds of thousands of athletes, so make sure yours captivates them. Once your mid-season highlight is complete, research coaches in your area and reach out to them. If they like what they see, build a relationship with them. Think of it this way: Scholarships are essentially money. If you were in a coach's shoes, would you rather give $50,000 to someone you know or to a complete stranger? This is why maintaining relationships with coaches is vital.

The Art of Coach Communication

Let me tell you something about college coaches: They can smell fake interest from a mile away. They get hundreds of basic emails that all sound the same:

Dear Coach,

I'm very interested in your program...

Delete. You need to stand out, not just in your film, but in how you approach these relationships.

Think about it from their perspective. Every day, they're flooded with messages from players, parents, and recruiting services. Why should they pay attention to yours? The answer isn't just about what you say; it's about how you say it, when you say it, and, most importantly, what you do after you say it.

Making First Contact Count

Your first message to a coach is like a first impression; you only get one shot. Here's what they want to see: that you've done your homework. Therefore, know something about their program. Maybe they run an offense that fits your skills perfectly. Maybe they've had success developing players at your position. Show them you've thought about why their program specifically makes sense for you.

Don't just tell them you're interested; show them why they should be interested in you. Lead with your best stats and most impressive achievements, but keep it short and clear. Coaches don't have time to read your life story in that first message.

Building Real Relationships

Here's the truth about recruiting: It's not about one big moment; it's about consistent, real communication over time. That means following up smart, not desperate. Update them on your progress. Share new achievements. Show them you're continuing to develop.

But here's the key: Make every contact count. Don't reach out just to reach out. Have a purpose. Whether sharing new highlights, updating them on your academic progress, or asking intelligent questions about their program, make sure you're adding value to the conversation.

The Follow-up Formula

Timing is everything in recruiting. Too much contact looks desperate. Too little looks disinterested. Find the sweet spot. When a coach responds to you, reply promptly but thoughtfully. Show them you respect their time while showing you really care.

Keep track of your communications. Know when you last reached out, what was discussed, and what the next steps should be. This isn't just about staying organized; it's about showing coaches you're detailed and professional in your approach.

Communication Do's and Don'ts

Let's talk about what works and what doesn't. I've seen players blow opportunities because they didn't understand the unwritten rules of recruiting communication.

Be authentic in your communication. Don't try to be someone you're not. Coaches have been doing this for years, so they can tell when a parent or coach is writing your emails. They want to hear your voice, understand your personality, and get a sense of who you really are.

Remember that everything you say or write can be shared. Be professional, be respectful, and be honest. If you're talking to multiple schools—which you should be—don't play games or try to create artificial pressure. The recruiting world is smaller than you think—coaches talk to each other.

The Long Game

Building relationships with coaches is a marathon, not a sprint. Some will respond quickly, others won't. Some will show intense interest, then cool off. Others might not show much interest initially but warm up over time. Stay consistent, stay professional, and stay patient.

Coaches aren't just evaluating your athletic ability but also how you handle yourself through this process. Show them you're mature, professional, and serious about their program. Every interaction is an opportunity to prove you're the type of player they want in their program.

Managing the Process

This process may sound straightforward, but it's complex. It won't always go smoothly. Coaches might leave you on read, stop communicating, or even turn you down. Don't take it personally. The goal is to find the school where you feel most comfortable and where the coach genuinely wants you. Don't just go where there's an open spot; go where you're wanted.

The Reality of Recruitment

Let me tell you about the side of recruiting nobody talks about. It's emotional. It's stressful. There will be days when you feel on top of the world because a dream school showed interest and days when you question everything because that same school suddenly goes quiet. This is normal. This is part of the process.

Think of recruiting like a full-time job because that's what it is essentially. You need to be organized, professional, and systematic in your approach. The players who succeed in recruiting aren't always the most talented; they're often the ones who manage the process the best.

Staying Organized Amid the Chaos

Your recruitment journey is like running multiple job applications at the same time. Each school has its own timeline, requirements, and way of doing things. Thus, you need to implement a system to keep track of everything.

Create a recruiting checklist for yourself. Track every interaction with every school. When did you last send a film? When did they respond? What feedback did they give? What are the next steps? This isn't about being obsessive; it's about being professional.

Don't rely on your memory. Write down everything. A coach might reference something from a conversation three months ago, and you need to know what they're talking about. Details matter in this process.

Planning Campus Visits

Campus visits are your chance to see beyond the highlight videos and recruiting pitches, but they require careful planning. When you visit a campus, you're not just evaluating facilities; you're evaluating your potential future home.

Make each visit count. Prepare questions ahead of time, not just about football but about academics, campus life, and player development. Watch how current players interact with coaches and how the program operates when they're not trying to impress recruits.

Remember: You're not just being evaluated during visits; you're doing the evaluating. Does this feel like a place where you can succeed? Can you see yourself here for four years? These aren't just football decisions; they're life decisions.

Managing Your Timeline

Recruiting doesn't follow a neat, predictable schedule. Different schools move at different speeds. Some might want a decision quickly; others might keep you waiting. You need to manage these varying timelines while keeping your options open.

Be strategic about your timeline. Early signing period? Regular signing period? Preferred walk-on opportunities? Each path has its own timeline and considerations. Don't let anyone pressure you into a decision before you're ready, but also understand that scholarships won't wait forever.

Making the Right Decision

Here's something crucial to understand: The *best* program isn't always the best program for you. A lower-division school where you'll play early might be better than a well-known program where you'll sit for three years. This is where your decision criteria become critical.

Think beyond the obvious factors. Yes, consider the level of play, the facilities, and the coaching staff, but also think about the following:

- the style of play and how it fits your skills
- the depth chart at your position
- the academic support for athletes
- the track record of player development
- the program's culture

When Things Don't Go as Planned

Here's a truth about recruiting: It rarely goes exactly as planned. Maybe your dream school doesn't make an offer. Maybe a coach who was recruiting you takes another job. Maybe an offer you were counting on goes to someone else.

This is where mental toughness comes in. Setbacks aren't failures; they're redirections. Some of the most successful college players ended up at schools that weren't initially on their radar. Stay flexible. Stay positive. Keep working.

Remember: You're not just choosing a football program; you're choosing a path for your future. Take control of this process. Stay organized. Stay professional. And most importantly, trust your instincts. When it's right, you'll know.

Handling Adversity

Let me tell you something nobody wants to talk about in recruiting: rejection. It's going to happen. Maybe not from every school, but it will happen. And how you handle these moments—these tests of your character—will define not just your recruiting journey but your future in football.

The Reality of Rejection

I've been there. That moment when a school you've been talking to for months suddenly goes quiet. Or when that offer you thought was coming doesn't happen. Or worse, when a coach looks you in the eye and says, "We're going in a different direction."

It hurts. It's supposed to hurt. If it didn't hurt, it would mean you didn't care enough. But here's what separates the players who make it from those who don't: their response to these moments.

Think about every great player you've ever heard of. I guarantee you they faced rejection somewhere along the line. Tom Brady was pick 199. Jerry Rice was overlooked by major programs. The list goes on. It's not about avoiding rejection; it's about using it as fuel.

Let me tell you another secret about rejection in football: It happens to everyone. That five-star recruit you follow on social media? He got told "no" by schools, too. That All-American you watch on Saturdays? There were coaches who didn't want him. That NFL Pro Bowler? He got cut from teams before making it big.

Here's what rejection really is:

- It's not a stop sign; it's a detour.

- It's not an ending – it's a redirect.

- It's not a judgment of your worth; it's just one program's decision at one moment in time.

- It's not a reason to quit; it's a reason to prove people wrong.

Managing Expectations

Here's a hard truth about recruiting: Your dreams might need to be adjusted, but they don't need to be abandoned. Maybe you won't play at that big SEC school you've dreamed about since you were a kid. But that doesn't mean you can't have an amazing college career somewhere else.

I've seen too many players ruin their chances by focusing so hard on their *dream school* that they miss other amazing opportunities. Every level of college football has produced NFL players. Every level has produced successful people in life after football.

Think about it like this: If your GPS app shows a road closure on your planned route, you don't just give up and go home. You find another way. Maybe it's not the route you planned. Maybe it takes a little longer. But you still get to your destination.

That's what this is about. Your dream isn't just to play at one specific school; your dream is to

- play college football.
- get your education.
- develop as a player.
- prepare for your future.
- make an impact.
- prove you belong.

And here's the thing: You can do *all* of that at many different schools. I've seen players turn D-II offers into NFL careers. I've seen guys go the *juco* route and end up at major programs. I've seen walk-ons become starters.

Set high goals, absolutely. But be realistic about your path to achieving them. Sometimes, the best route to where you want to go isn't a straight line. Sometimes, you need to take a different path to get to your destination.

It's not about where you start; it's about where you finish. And more importantly, it's about what you do with the opportunities you get. Because at the end of the day, it only takes one school to believe in you. One chance to prove yourself. One opportunity to show what you can do.

Staying Motivated Through Adversity

Let me tell you how to stay motivated when things get tough. First, remember why you started. Not just your love of football but what the game means to you, what it's taught you, and where it can take you.

Create small wins for yourself. Maybe you didn't get that offer you wanted, but did you improve your forty time? Did you raise your GPA? Did you perfect that route you've been working on? Progress isn't always about offers and commitments. Sometimes, it's about the small improvements that make you a better player and person.

Keep working. The worst thing you can do when facing adversity is to stop. Don't let a rejection stop your training. Don't let a "no" keep you from sending out more film. Don't let disappointment keep you from improving.

Finding Alternative Paths

Sometimes, you need to get creative in your journey. Maybe the traditional recruiting path isn't working. That's when you need to look at alternatives:

Junior College isn't the end of your dreams; it's often a rebirth. Some of the greatest players in football history went the juco route. It's not about where you start; it's about where you finish.

Walk-on opportunities can be golden if you have the right mindset. Being a walk-on means you have to work harder, be tougher, and want it more than anyone else. But guess what? Coaches notice that kind of dedication.

Division II and III programs often offer amazing opportunities for playing time and development. And here's something people don't talk about enough: Many of these programs have excellent academic support and career placement rates.

The Mental Game

Your mind will be your greatest ally or worst enemy during this process. You'll face doubt from others and yourself. You'll have moments where you question everything. This is normal. This is part of the journey.

Build your mental toughness like you build your physical strength: gradually, consistently, and deliberately. Every setback is an opportunity to prove your strength. Every rejection is a chance to show your character.

The Bigger Picture

Remember this: Recruiting is just one chapter in your football story. It's important, yes, but it's not the end-all-be-all. Some of the most successful players in football history had difficult recruiting journeys.

Stay focused on what you can control. Keep improving. Keep working. Keep believing. Because at the end of the day, it's not about how many offers you get; it's about making the most of the opportunities that do come your way.

The road might be harder than you expected. The path might be different than you planned. But if you stay dedicated, focused, and true to yourself, you'll find your way. Sometimes, the best stories are the ones with the most plot twists.

Making the Right Choice

Let me tell you about the biggest mistake I see recruits make: Choosing a school for the wrong reasons. They pick the biggest name, where their friends are going, or just because it's a Division I program. But here's the truth: The right choice isn't about the school's ranking or its football reputation. It's about where you'll thrive, both as a player and a person.

Understanding Program Fit

Think about this like finding the right position in football. Just because someone's a great athlete doesn't mean they should play quarterback.

Just because a school has a great football program doesn't mean it's great for you.

When I chose between Saskatchewan and Calgary, it wasn't just about football. Saskatchewan was offering immediate playing time, but Calgary offered competition and growth. I knew I needed to be pushed, to be challenged. I needed a program that would force me to become better, not just give me what I wanted right away.

Your program fit goes beyond the depth chart. How does the offensive or defensive scheme match your skills? Does it have a history of developing players at your position? Is it known for giving young players a chance to earn playing time? These aren't just questions; they're your future.

Think about it like choosing the right shoes for game day. Sure, those flashy ones might look good, but if they don't fit right, you can't perform your best. The same goes for choosing a program. The big-name school might look impressive, but if it's not the right fit, you won't reach your full potential.

Here's what a real program fit looks like:

- It's where the coaching style matches how you learn best.

- It's where the system lets you use your strengths.

- It's where the culture pushes you to grow.

- It's where you can see yourself getting better every day.

- It's where you feel challenged but not overwhelmed.

- It's where you're valued, not just tolerated.

Remember my story: Saskatchewan was offering what I wanted—playing time—but Calgary was offering what I needed—competition and growth. Sometimes, the best fit isn't the easiest path. Sometimes, it's the path that's going to push you, challenge you, and force you to level up.

Look beyond the surface. Watch how coaches interact with players during practice. See how players support each other on the sidelines. Ask yourself: *Can I see myself here not just on game days but during those tough Monday practices? Not just during wins, but during losses? Not just during my best moments, but during my struggles?*

The right fit isn't about picking the biggest name or the easiest path. It's about finding the place where you can grow not just as a player but as a person.

The Development Factor

Here's something crucial to understand: College is about development, not just playing time. Look at the program's track record. How many players at your position have they developed? What's their strength and conditioning program like? What kind of coaching stability do they have?

The best program for you is one that can take you from where you are to where you want to be. Maybe that's a Power 5 school with NFL-level facilities. Maybe it's a smaller program where you'll get more individual attention. The key is finding a place that will invest in your development.

Academic and Cultural Alignment

Football will end someday. Whether after college or after a long NFL career, you need to think about life beyond the game. Does the school have strong programs in what you want to study? What's their graduation rate for athletes? What kind of academic support do they provide?

The culture of the program will be your daily reality, so make sure it's a family you want to be part of.

The Decision Process

Since this is a life decision, it is better to do the following:
- Take your time with this decision.
- Visit the schools if you can.
- Talk to current players.
- Research the coaches' backgrounds.
- Look at the town or city you'll be living in.

The right choice isn't always the most obvious one. Sometimes, the best opportunity isn't at the biggest school or the most prestigious program. It's where you'll have the best chance to grow, develop, and succeed—both on and off the field.

The Final Message

All in all, this chapter held invaluable information. Use it not just in your football career but throughout your life. If you follow these steps and check off every box, you will be successful. Remember, no one will be there to push you to do what's necessary. You have to look yourself in the mirror every night and be honest about whether you gave it everything or held back. This game is not for the weak; it's a man's game. Just like in life, men don't get sympathy. Coaches don't care if you're tired or hurting; everyone is. Everyone's sore and mentally dealing with challenges. The cream of the crop rises above all of this and commits to being the best every single day, not just when they feel like it.

Whatever your goals are, they're possible. Have faith in God, believe in yourself, and put in the work. No one can do it for you. Remember, success is *earned*, not given.

Beyond Recruitment

Let me tell you something important about everything we've covered in this chapter: These lessons go far beyond football recruitment. Marketing yourself, building relationships, handling rejection, and making tough decisions are all life skills that will serve you long after your playing days are over.

Think about it. The same process of putting yourself out there for college coaches? That's not so different from job hunting. Building relationships with recruiters? That's like building connections that will help you succeed later in life. Handling rejection and staying motivated? That's starting your own business. Making a major life decision? That's something you'll do multiple times in your career.

The recruiting process isn't just about finding a place to play football; it's about learning how to navigate life's biggest challenges and opportunities. The skills you're developing now, the resilience you're building, and the professional habits you're forming will be your toolkit for success in whatever path you choose.

This chapter wasn't just about getting recruited. It was about becoming the kind of person who succeeds, no matter what challenges life throws your way.

Conclusion

You've made it this far. You've committed to learning, growing, and understanding what it really takes to succeed in this game. But here's what you might not realize yet: Everything you've learned in these pages? It's about so much more than football.

Think about what you've absorbed. The mindset of a champion. The discipline of a scholar. The work ethic of a professional. The strategy of a recruiter. These aren't just football lessons; they're life lessons wrapped in shoulder pads and cleats.

Every drill you run, every class you ace, and every early morning workout you crush are all building something bigger than a football career. They're building you. The you that will succeed not just on the field, but in boardrooms, business ventures, and life's biggest moments.

I've seen it happen. Players who took these lessons and became successful entrepreneurs. Athletes who applied this mindset to become community leaders. Young men who used these principles to build legacies far beyond their playing days.

This book isn't just a guide to football success; it's your blueprint for life. The same fire that drives you to be great on the field? That's the fire that will drive you to excellence in everything you do. The discipline that makes you study film? That's the discipline that will make you master your craft, whatever it may be.

You're not just building an athlete. You're building a future leader, a future success story, and a future force for change in this world.

Are you ready to take these lessons beyond the game?

The Mindset of Champions

Remember how we started this journey? That conversation about mindset, about believing in yourself when nobody else does, about seeing your future so clearly that nothing could shake your faith? That wasn't just about football

Think back to that story I shared about being told I'd never make it to the NFL. About that moment when someone tried to "be realistic" with my dreams. How many times in life will you face that same challenge? How many times will someone tell you to lower your expectations, to settle for less, to "be realistic?"

But here's what champions understand: Reality isn't fixed. Reality is what you make it. Every great achievement in human history started with someone being *unrealistic*. Every breakthrough began with someone believing in something others thought impossible.

The mental toughness that you develop in football? That's your secret weapon in life. When your business faces setbacks, when your career hits obstacles, when life throws you curveballs... that's when this mindset becomes your armor. The ability to get knocked down and get back up, to face adversity and keep pushing forward, to believe in your vision when others doubt... that's not just athlete mentality; that's the champion's mentality.

I've seen former players use this mindset to build successful companies. I've watched teammates transform into influential leaders. The common thread? They understood that the champion's mindset isn't confined to the field. They took the mental toughness that football demanded and applied it to every challenge they faced.

When you're grinding through those early morning workouts, you're not just building physical strength; you're building mental resilience. When you're pushing through that extra rep when your body's screaming to stop, you're not just developing athletic endurance; you're developing life endurance. When you're studying film, analyzing plays, and learning from mistakes, you're not just becoming a better player; you're becoming a better learner, leader, and person.

This mindset, this unwavering belief in yourself, this relentless pursuit of excellence, this ability to rise above challenges... this is your true competitive advantage in life. Because long after the cheers fade and the lights go dark, this mindset will continue to drive you toward new goals, new achievements, and new victories.

Remember: Champions aren't born on game day. They're forged in the quiet moments of dedication, the daily choices to pursue excellence, and the consistent commitment to their vision. And that kind of champion? They're unstoppable in any arena they choose.

Life's Playbook

Think of everything we've covered as your playbook for success—not just in football, but in life. Each chapter wasn't just about becoming a better athlete; it was about becoming a better version of yourself.

The Foundation of Excellence

Remember what we learned about academics? That wasn't just about staying eligible or getting recruited. That was about understanding that true success requires a complete dedication to excellence. Those late nights studying, those extra hours in the library, that commitment to mastering subjects you might not love, that was preparing you for life's bigger challenges.

Think about what you've really been learning:

- When you pushed through that tough math assignment? You were learning to solve problems under pressure.

- When you balanced football and finals? You were learning to handle multiple responsibilities.

- When you asked teachers for help? You were learning to seek guidance when needed.

- When you stayed up late to finish a project? You were building a work ethic.

The discipline it takes to maintain your grades while pursuing athletic excellence? That's the same discipline you'll need when balancing a career, family, and personal goals. The ability to focus in the classroom when you're tired from practice? That's the same focus you'll need in any challenging situation life throws at you.

Education isn't just about grades; it's about developing your mind as thoroughly as you develop your body. It's about building the mental strength that will carry you through life's toughest moments. Every test you study for, every paper you write, and every challenge you overcome in the classroom are all preparation for the bigger games ahead.

The Power of Process

Think about our training discussions. The commitment to showing up every day, the dedication to proper form, and the understanding that real progress takes time aren't just workout principles; they form the blueprint for success in anything you pursue.

Remember those early morning workouts? Those were about more than getting stronger. They were about

- keeping promises to yourself
- doing what needs to be done, even when you don't feel like it
- understanding that great achievements come from daily habits
- building the strength to pursue your dreams when others are sleeping

Want to be successful in anything? You'll need that same consistent effort, attention to detail, and patience with the process. The habits you've built in training—showing up early, giving extra effort, never cutting corners—will set you apart in whatever you choose to do.

The Championship Mindset

The mindset of a champion isn't just for game day. It's for every day:
- When others quit, you persist.
- When others rest, you work.
- When others make excuses, you make progress.
- When others look for shortcuts, you embrace the journey.

Think about what you've really gained from this journey:
- the confidence to face any challenge
- the strength to push through adversity
- the wisdom to learn from setbacks
- the courage to chase big dreams
- the discipline to do what others won't
- the heart to never give up

The habits you've built in training—discipline, persistence, relentless pursuit of improvement—are your competitive advantages in life. In a world where many people look for shortcuts, you understand the value of putting in the work.

Remember: Life, like football, rewards those who prepare. Those who show up. Those who put in the work when no one's watching. You've learned these lessons on the field and in the classroom. Now, it's time to apply them to every area of your life.

Your playbook for success is written. The question is: Are you ready to run the plays?

The Art of Opportunity

And remember what you learned about recruitment? That wasn't just about getting college offers. That was about understanding how to present yourself, build meaningful relationships, and stand out in a competitive field. These are skills that will serve you in every professional endeavor you pursue.

The ability to market yourself to coaches? That's how you'll sell yourself to employers, clients, or investors. The persistence in building relationships with recruiters? That's how you'll network and build professional connections. The resilience in handling rejection? That's how you'll navigate the ups and downs of any career path.

These aren't separate lessons; they're all parts of the same success story. Your story. The story of someone who understands that excellence isn't just about what you do on the field; it's about how you approach every aspect of your life.

Beyond the Field

Look around at the most successful people in any field—business leaders, entrepreneurs, community champions. You'll notice something interesting: Many of them played sports, and a lot of them played football. This isn't a coincidence. The principles that make you great on the field are the same principles that drive success in every arena of life.

Leadership Born in Battle

Think about what football teaches you about leadership. When you're down in the fourth quarter, when you need to rally your teammates, when you have to perform under pressure... these moments are preparing you for bigger stages. Every time you lead by example in practice, every time you lift up a teammate who's struggling, and every time you put the team's success before your own glory, you're developing leadership skills that will set you apart in any field you choose.

I've seen former players become CEOs, leading companies with the same principles they learned on the field. I've watched teammates become community leaders, using the same ability to unite people toward a common goal they used in the huddle. The leadership lessons you're learning now? They're preparing you for moments you can't even imagine yet.

The Ultimate Team Sport

Football teaches you something crucial about success: Nobody does it alone. Just like you need your offensive line to make plays, just like you need your receivers to run the right routes, you'll need to build and work with teams throughout your life. The ability to work within a team, understand your role, and put collective success above individual glory is a quality that employers crave, successful businesses require, and meaningful achievements demand.

Rising Above

Every adversity you face on the field is preparing you for life's bigger challenges. That injury you fought back from? That's resilience. That game plan that failed, forcing you to adjust? That's adaptability. That tough loss that you bounced back from? That's perseverance. These aren't just athletic qualities; they're success principles that will serve you in everything you do.

Your Bigger Impact

But here's what's really exciting: Everything you're learning now is preparing you to make a real difference in the world. The discipline, leadership, and ability to bounce back aren't just tools for personal success. They're tools for creating positive change in your community, lifting others up, and making an impact that goes far beyond personal achievement.

Think about the players who've inspired you, the ones who really made a difference. Sure, they were great athletes, but that's not why people remember them. They're remembered because they used football as a launching pad to do something bigger. They started youth programs. They built community centers. They went back to their neighborhoods and created opportunities for the next generation.

This game gives you a platform, but what you do with that platform is the real test of character. Will you use these lessons to just build your own success, or will you use them to create opportunities for others? Will you be content with personal achievement, or will you strive to be a force for positive change in your community?

Look at the greats who came before you. Walter Payton wasn't just a Hall of Fame running back; he was a champion for charity work. Jerry Rice didn't just catch touchdowns; he caught kids before they fell through the cracks, giving them hope and opportunity. These legends understood that their real legacy wasn't just about yards and touchdowns but the lives they changed.

You're learning more than just how to read defenses and run routes. You're learning how to:

- lead when times are tough
- lift others up when they're down
- stand strong when facing challenges
- build something bigger than yourself
- make decisions that impact others
- create change when change is needed

Every drill you run, every weight you lift, and every play you study are all preparing you for something bigger. Maybe you'll be the one who starts a youth program in your hometown. Maybe you'll be the one who helps kids see college as a real possibility. Maybe you'll be the one who comes back and shows the next generation what's possible.

Remember: The biggest game you'll ever play isn't on any field. It's the game of life, and everything you're learning now is preparing you to win that game. But winning isn't just about personal success; it's about how many others you help win along the way.

Football isn't just teaching you how to be a better player. It's teaching you how to be a leader, a mentor, a change-maker. The question isn't whether you'll have the tools to make a difference—you will. The question is: What difference will you choose to make?

Your journey in football is just the beginning. The real victory? That comes from what you do with everything this game has taught you. That's your true legacy. That's your biggest play. That's your real touchdown.

Your Time Is Now

Listen up because this might be the most important thing you'll read in this entire book: Everything you want to achieve—every dream, every goal, every vision you have for your future—comes down to what you decide to do right now. Not tomorrow. Not next week. Now.

You've got the blueprint. You've got the knowledge. You've got the understanding of what it takes. But none of that matters if you don't take action. The clock is ticking, and unlike a football game, you don't get to call a time-out in life to figure things out.

The Power of Now

Every single day, you're making choices that either move you closer to your dreams or further away from them. Every time you choose the easy path over the right path, every time you let "I'll do it tomorrow" become your excuse, and every time you settle for less than your best, you're choosing your future.

Think about that for a second. The choices you make today—whether to study or slack off, whether to put in extra work or call it early, whether to push through discomfort or give in to comfort—aren't just daily decisions. They're laying the foundation for who you'll become.

Building Your Legacy

Your legacy isn't something that starts when you make it big. Your legacy is being built right now, in the quiet moments when nobody's watching. It's being built through the decisions you make when it would be easier to take shortcuts. It's being built in how you handle adversity, how you treat others, and how you pursue excellence even when nobody's keeping score.

Ten years from now, people won't remember every tackle you made or every touchdown you scored. But they will remember your character. They will remember your work ethic. They will remember how you carried yourself in victory and defeat. They will remember the impact you had on others.

The question isn't whether you have what it takes. The question is: Are you willing to do what it takes? Are you ready to be accountable to your dreams? Are you prepared to make the daily choices that champions make?

Your time is now. What are you going to do with it?

The Final Challenge

This is it. The moment where everything we've discussed becomes real. I've given you every tool, every insight, and every lesson I've learned on my journey. But now, it's your turn. Now, it's time to take everything you've learned and turn it into action.

Here's your challenge: Start today—not tomorrow, not next week, but today—and commit to excellence in everything you do. Whether you're in the weight room or the classroom, whether you're watching film or studying for a test, whether you're practicing routes or preparing for your future, give it everything you've got.

Don't wait for the perfect moment. Don't wait until you feel ready. Don't wait for someone to push you. The greatest achievements in life came from people willing to start before they felt ready, to push themselves when nobody was watching, and to believe in themselves when others doubted.

Take what you've learned in these pages and make it your reality. Set those goals we talked about. Create that schedule we discussed. Build those habits we outlined. Start that journey we mapped out. But most importantly, commit to seeing it through.

Champions aren't born. They're not discovered. They're not created by luck or circumstance. Champions are built—decision by decision, day by day, commitment by commitment.

Your journey starts now. Your future is waiting. Your legacy is yours to build.

What are you going to do about it?

The choice is yours. The time is now.

Let's get to work.

References

Allen, T. (2023, March 15). *Recruiting for football: The ultimate guide.* GMTM. https://gmtm.com/articles/recruiting-for-football-the-ultimate-guid

Anzilotti, A. (2019). *Safety tips: Football (for teens).* Kids Health. https://kidshealth.org/en/teens/safety-football.html

Armetta, B. (2021, August 10). *How does recruiting work in today's CFB landscape?* GMTM. https://gmtm.com/articles/how-recruiting-works-in-college-football-2021

Coach Horton. (2023). *Football strength training (a complete guide).* Horton Barbell. https://hortonbarbell.com/football-strength-training-a-complete-guide

College football recruiting guide: How to get recruited. (2023, July 22). College Openings. https://collegeopenings.com/college-football-recruiting-guide-how-to-get-recruited-and-secure-scholarships

Daily Editorials. (2023, September 5). *Football remains America's most popular high school sport.* Creators. https://www.creators.com/read/daily-editorials/09/23/football-remains-americas-most-popular-high-school-sport-4e1c6

Degnan, J. (2023, November 22). *Report predicts 72% of all US jobs will require postsecondary education by 2031.* New Jersey Business & Industry Association. https://njbia.org/report-predicts-72-of-all-us-jobs-will-require-postsecondary-education-by-2031/

Derek Carr's football safety tips for teens. (2024). Valley Children's Healthcare. https://www.valleychildrens.org/blog/derek-carrs-football-safety-tips-for-teens

Egan, E. (2023, March 31). *Fact check: Do college graduates earn $1 million more over a lifetime than high school graduates?* WRAL.

https://www.wral.com/story/fact-check-do-college-graduates-earn-1-million-more-over-a-lifetime-than-high-school-graduates/20783647/

5 stages of college recruiting process. (2023, February 28). GMTM. https://gmtm.com/articles/5-stages-of-college-recruiting-process

Football mental toughness. (2012). Sport Psychology Today. https://www.sportpsychologytoday.com/youth-sports-psychology/football-mental-toughness

Football workout: The ultimate guide to turn into an athletic monster. (2022). 5 Star Football Package. https://www.5starfootballpackage.com/fb-blogs/ultimate-football-training-guide

45 football drills for all ages, skill levels, and positions. (n.d.). Football Advantage. https://footballadvantage.com/football-drills

Gardiner, C. (n.d.). *Mental toughness: Nature vs. nurture?* BelievePerform. https://members.believeperform.com/mental-toughness-nature-vs-nurture

Gill, G. (n.d.). *Mental toughness in football.* BelievePerform. https://members.believeperform.com/mental-toughness-in-football

Hall, B. (2022). *8 football drills for building NFL-style speed and explosiveness.* Stack. https://www.stack.com/a/8-football-drills-for-building-nfl-style-speed-and-explosiveness

How athletes use visualization to enhance performance. (2024, August 16). *Lumende Blog.* https://lumende.com/blog/how-athletes-use-visualization-to-enhance-performance/

How does a college degree improve graduates' employment and earnings potential? (2022). APLU. https://www.aplu.org/our-work/4-policy-and-advocacy/publicuvalues/employment-earnings/

How to catch a football. (n.d.). NFL Flag. https://nflflag.com/coaches/football-drills/how-to-catch-a-football

Martin, C. (n.d.). *45 football drills for all ages, skill levels, and positions.* Football Advantage. https://footballadvantage.com/football-drills

Motivation: 8 common sense tips from Bob Ladouceur. (2003, June). American Football Monthly. https://www.americanfootballmonthly.com/Arena/sections/staffrep/03june/motivation.html

Navigating college football recruiting. (2024, January 18). JMC Recruiting. https://jmcrecruiting.com/navigating-college-football-recruiting

NEED, P. (2024, May 24). *1st time football players NEED TO KNOW THIS (8 tips)* [Video]. YouTube. https://youtu.be/Z2LPmySQHUI

NFL way to play. (n.d.). NFL Play Football. https://playfootball.nfl.com/nfl-way-to-play/tips-for-players/

Ronglan, L. T., & Feddersen, N. B. (2021, December 15). Recruitment in elite football: A network approach. *European Sport Management Quarterly.* https://www.tandfonline.com/doi/pdf/10.1080/16184742.2021.2011942

Schlinger, A. (2023, April 7). *American football 101: How to play the game.* Nike.com. https://www.nike.com/a/how-to-play-football

30 most inspirational football quotes. (2023, August 5). Athlon Sports. https://athlonsports.com/college-football/inspirational-football-quotes

Top 10 exercises for football strength and speed. (2018, May 2). American Football International. https://www.americanfootballinternational.com/top-10-exercises-football-strength-speed

Training techniques for football: Boost your game with top drills & tips. (2023, March 15). Huff Sports. https://huffsports.com/football/training-techniques-for-football

Image References

Adamson, D. (2019, August 23). *Brown rugby ball* [Image]. Unsplash. https://unsplash.com/photos/brown-rugby-ball-0Z4ghx_P3q4

Al-zayat, R. (2016, December 2). *Silver Android smartphone* [Image]. Unsplash. https://unsplash.com/photos/silver-android-smartphone-w33-zg-dNL4

Basheer, A. (2019, May 6). *Football field during daytime* [Image]. Unsplash. https://unsplash.com/photos/two-footballs-sitting-on-a-football-field-at-sunset-bbkIbELRxvM

Dumlao, N. (2020, February 27). *Clear plastic bottle* [Image]. Unsplash. https://unsplash.com/photos/person-holding-clear-plastic-bottle-CHaIF4oJRtI

Félix, A. (2018, February 5). *Person writing on paper leaning on brown table* [Image]. Unsplash. https://unsplash.com/photos/person-writing-on-paper-leaning-on-brown-table-Yi9-QIObQ1o

Gallin, G. (2021, October 15). *A close-up of a football helmet on the field* [Image]. Unsplash. https://unsplash.com/photos/a-close-up-of-a-football-helmet-on-the-field-wMiAjt0qfzk

Habeshaw, G. (2018, June 11). *Man sitting on concrete bench reading book* [Image]. Unsplash. https://unsplash.com/photos/man-sitting-on-concrete-bench-reading-book-eR0dgeG1wqY

Nascimento, B. (2019, October 14). *Orange and gray Nike shoes walking on gray concrete stairs* [Image]. Unsplash.

https://unsplash.com/photos/person-wearing-orange-and-gray-nike-shoes-walking-on-gray-concrete-stairs-PHIgYUGQPvU

Petrik, R. (2024, June 27). *Two footballs sitting on a football field at sunset* [Image]. Unsplash. https://unsplash.com/photos/two-footballs-sitting-on-a-football-field-at-sunset-bbkIbELRxvM